Architecture, Analysis, and Design

BUILDING THE

UNSTRUCTURED

DATA WAREHOUSE

first edition

Architecture, Analysis, and Design

BUILDING THE

UNSTRUCTURED

DATA WAREHOUSE

first edition

W. H. Inmon

Krish Krishnan

Technics Publications

New Jersey

Published by:

Technics Publications, LLC
Post Office Box 161
Bradley Beach, NJ 07720 U.S.A.
www.technicspub.com

Edited by Carol Lehn

Cover design by Mark Brye

Cartoons by Abby Denson, www.abbycomix.com

ISBN, print ed.   978-1-9355040-4-7
ISBN, ePub ed.   978-1-9355043-3-7
ISBN, Kindle ed.   978-1-9355043-4-4

First Printing 2011
Library of Congress Control Number: 2010938989

ATTENTION SCHOOLS AND BUSINESSES: Technics Publications books are available at quantity discounts with bulk purchase for educational, business, or sales promotional use. For information, please write to Technics Publications, PO Box 161, Bradley Beach, NJ 07090, or email Steve Hoberman, President of Technics Publications, at me@stevehoberman.com.

To Steve Hitchman and Jackie Harper - my Australian friends and inspirations.

— William Inmon

To my parents, my family and my teachers. Without you this would not be possible.

— Krish Krishnan

Contents at a Glance

Introduction _____ *15*

SECTION I: Unstructured Data Warehouse Essentials _____ *17*

CHAPTER 1: Exploring our Unstructured World _____ *19*

CHAPTER 2: Managing Unstructured Data _____ *27*

CHAPTER 3: Evolving to the Unstructured Data Warehouse _____ *39*

CHAPTER 4: Extracting, Transforming, and Loading Text _____ *67*

CHAPTER 5: Developing the Unstructured Data Warehouse _____ *99*

SECTION II: Unstructured Data Warehouse Advanced Topics _____ *109*

CHAPTER 6: Inventorying and Linking Text _____ *111*

CHAPTER 7: Using Indexes _____ *121*

CHAPTER 8: Leveraging Taxonomies _____ *141*

CHAPTER 9: Coping with Large Amounts of Data _____ *153*

Chapter 10: Selecting Technology _____ *165*

SECTION III: Unstructured Data Warehouse Case Studies _____ *187*

CHAPTER 11: The Ablatz Medical Group _____ *189*

CHAPTER 12: The Eastern Hills Oil Company _____ *199*

CHAPTER 13: The Amber Oil Company _____ *203*

Suggested Reading _____ *211*

Index _____ *213*

Contents

Introduction _____ *15*

*SECTION I: Unstructured Data Warehouse Essentials*_____ *17*

CHAPTER 1: Exploring our Unstructured World _____ *19*

  Text Form _____ **21**
    Documents _____21
    Email _____21
    Spreadsheets _____22
    Embedded Text_____22

  Text Characteristics _____ **23**
    Homogeneity _____23
    Format _____24
    Medium _____24
    Volume _____24
    Structure_____25

CHAPTER 2: Managing Unstructured Data _____ *27*

  Volume_____ **27**

  Blather _____ **28**

  The Tower of Babel _____ **30**

  Spelling_____ **31**

  Lack of Natural Relationships _____ **32**

  Storage Format _____ **33**

  Data Junkyards_____ **34**

  Paper _____ **36**

CHAPTER 3: Evolving to the Unstructured Data Warehouse _____ *39*

  We Have Come a Long Way_____ **40**

  Caught in the Spider's Web _____ **41**

  Data Warehouse to the Rescue_____ **42**

  Data Warehouse 2.0 to the Rescue_____ **46**
    Unstructured Components_____49

Unstructured Data Warehouse to the Rescue _____ 49

The Thematic Approach_____ 55

Advantages Over a Traditional Search Engine _____ 56

Leveraging the Traditional Data Warehouse_____ 57

ETL Processing _____ 57

Integration _____ 59

Iteration _____ 62

*CHAPTER 4: Extracting, Transforming, and Loading Text*_____ 67

Extracting Text (The 'E' of ETL)_____ 69

Knowing the Source_____ 69

Reading Documents Only Once _____ 72

Identifying Common File Types _____ 72

Acquiring the "Read" Interface _____ 73

Transforming Text (The 'T' of ETL) _____ 77

Words and Phrases _____ 78

Stop Words _____ 79

Case _____ 79

Punctuation _____ 80

Font _____ 81

Stem_____ 81

Synonym Replacement _____ 82

Alternate Spelling_____ 83

Conceptual Abstractions _____ 83

Homographic Resolution _____ 84

Negativity Exclusion_____ 84

Inline Additions _____ 84

Recognizing Extensions of a Concept_____ 85

Patterns _____ 86

Proximity Analysis _____ 86

Clustering_____ 87

Loading Text (The 'L' of ETL) _____ 87

Using the Move/Remove Utility_____ 87

Reviewing the Output Tables_____ 89

Knowing the Final Destination_____ 89

Managing Volumes of Data _____ 90

Performing Checkpoint Processing _____ 91

Textual ETL Examples _____ 91
   Email _____91
   Spreadsheets _____94

CHAPTER 5: Developing the Unstructured Data Warehouse _____ **_99_**

  SDLC _____ 99

  Spiral Approach _____ 100

  Hybrid Approach _____ 100
   1. Understand the business problem and business context_____101
   2. Survey the data sources to determine which data is useful_____101
   3. Select and customize taxonomies_____102
   4. Select the initial set of data _____102
   5. Determine future iterations and source document requirements_____103
   6. Choose the textual ETL tool _____103
   7. Load parameters for transformations _____104
   8. Execute ETL scripts with initial set of data _____105
   9. Examine results and make adjustments if needed _____105
   10. Execute ETL scripts on remaining iterations_____105
   11. Continuous business analysis and make adjustments if needed _____106

  Putting the Steps Together _____ 106

SECTION II: Unstructured Data Warehouse Advanced Topics _____ **_109_**

_CHAPTER 6: Inventorying and Linking Text______ **_111_**

  Document Inventory _____ 111

  Document Classification _____ 113

  Linking Unstructured to Structured Data _____ 114
   A Probabilistic Linkage _____116
   Dynamic Linkages _____118
   Static Linkages _____119
   Dynamic versus Static _____119

CHAPTER 7: Using Indexes _____ **_121_**

  Simple Index_____ 123

  Fractured Index _____ 124

  Named Value Index _____ 126

  Taxonomy (or External Categorization) Index _____ 128

Patterned Index _____ 130

Homographic Index _____ 131

Alternate Spelling Index _____ 132

Stemmed Words Index _____ 132

Clustered Index _____ 133

Combined Index _____ 134

Leverage Multiple Indexing Strategies _____ 135

Semistructured (Sub Doc) Processing _____ 135

CHAPTER 8: Leveraging Taxonomies _____ 141

Simple Taxonomy _____ 142

Pairs of Words _____ 143

Preferred Taxonomy _____ 145

External Categorization _____ 146

Real World Problems _____ 147

Hierarchies Within the Taxonomy _____ 147

Multiple Types Within the Taxonomy _____ 148

Recursion Within the Taxonomy _____ 148

Relationships Between Taxonomies _____ 149

Taxonomies and Data Modeling _____ 149

CHAPTER 9: Coping with Large Amounts of Data _____ 153

Keeping Unstructured Data in Place _____ 154

Implementing Backward Pointers _____ 155

Doing Iterative Development _____ 156

Avoiding Rework _____ 157

Screening Data _____ 157

Removing Extraneous Data _____ 158

Selecting Appropriate Index Types _____ 159

Parallelizing the Workload _____ 160

Building Small Logically Related Tables _____ 161

Dividing Data into Sectors _____ 161

Chapter 10: Selecting Technology _____ **165**

Processing Structured Data _____ 165

Data Warehouse Performance _____167

Processing Unstructured Data _____ 169

Data Warehouse Appliance _____ 173

Appliance Architecture _____174

Data Distribution _____176

Workload _____177

Best Practices for Implementing Data Warehouse Appliances _____179

Using the Data Warehouse Appliance to build the Unstructured Database ___180

Example of Processing Unstructured Data _____183

SECTION III: Unstructured Data Warehouse Case Studies _____ **187**

CHAPTER 11: The Ablatz Medical Group _____ **189**

Information Systems _____ 189

Special Treatment Collections _____ 191

Users _____ 191

Integration _____ 192

Unstructured Text _____ 193

Sources of Data _____ 194

Textual Operating Parameters _____ 196

Visualization _____ 197

CHAPTER 12: The Eastern Hills Oil Company _____ **199**

CHAPTER 13: The Amber Oil Company _____ **203**

Maximizing Search Engines _____ 207

Legacy Search _____207

Relevancy Rankings _____209

Suggested Reading _____ **211**

Index _____ **213**

Answers for many valuable business questions hide in text. How well can your existing reporting environment extract the necessary text from email, spreadsheets, and documents, and put it in a useful format for analytics and reporting? Transforming the traditional data warehouse into an efficient *unstructured data warehouse* requires additional skills from the analyst, architect, designer, and developer.

This book will take you through three sections with the goal of preparing you to successfully implement an unstructured data warehouse and, through clear explanations, examples, and case studies, you will learn new techniques and tips to successfully obtain and analyze text.

Section I covers the foundation in terminology and techniques for building the unstructured data warehouse. Specifically, by the end of this section you will master these objectives:

- Build an unstructured data warehouse using the 11-step approach
- Integrate text and describe it in terms of homogeneity, relevance, medium, volume, and structure
- Overcome challenges, including blather, the Tower of Babel, and lack of natural relationships
- Avoid the Data Junkyard and combat the "Spider's Web"
- Reuse techniques perfected in the traditional data warehouse and Data Warehouse 2.0, including iterative development
- Apply essential techniques for textual Extract, Transform, and Load (ETL), such as phrase recognition, stop word filtering, and synonym replacement.

Section II covers more advanced topics on building the unstructured data warehouse. Specifically, by the end of this section, you will master these objectives:

- Design the Document Inventory system and link unstructured text to structured data

- Leverage indexes for efficient text analysis and taxonomies for useful external categorization
- Manage large volumes of data using advanced techniques, such as the use of backward pointers
- Evaluate technology choices suitable for unstructured data processing, such as data warehouse appliances.

Section III puts all of the previously discussed techniques and approaches in context through three case studies: the Ablatz Medical Group, the Eastern Hills Oil Company, and the Amber Oil Company.

SECTION I
Unstructured Data Warehouse Essentials

This section covers the foundation in terminology and techniques for building the unstructured data warehouse. Specifically, by the end of this section you will master these objectives:

- Build an unstructured data warehouse using the 11-step approach
- Integrate text and describe it in terms of homogeneity, relevance, medium, volume, and structure
- Overcome challenges, including blather, the Tower of Babel, and lack of natural relationships
- Avoid the Data Junkyard and combat the "Spider's Web"
- Reuse techniques perfected in the traditional data warehouse and Data Warehouse 2.0, including iterative development
- Apply essential techniques for textual Extract, Transform, and Load (ETL), such as phrase recognition, stop word filtering, and synonym replacement.

Chapter 1 defines unstructured data and explains why text is the main focus of this book. The sources for text, including documents, email, and spreadsheets, are described in terms of factors such as homogeneity, relevance, and structure.

Chapter 2 addresses the challenges one faces when managing unstructured data. These challenges include volume, blather, the Tower of Babel, spelling, and lack of natural relationships. Learn how to avoid a data junkyard, which occurs when unstructured data is not properly integrated into the data warehouse. This chapter emphasizes the importance of storing integrated unstructured data in a relational structure. We are cautioned on both the commonality and dangers associated with text based on paper.

Chapter 3 begins with a timeline of applications, highlighting their evolution over the decades. Eventually, powerful yet siloed applications created a "spider's web" environment. This chapter describes how data warehouses solved many problems, including the creation of corporate data, the ability to get out of the maintenance backlog conundrum, and greater data integrity and data accessibility. There were problems, however, with the data warehouse that were addressed in Data Warehouse 2.0 (DW 2.0), such as the inevitable data lifecycle. This chapter discusses the DW 2.0 architecture, which leads into the role of the unstructured data warehouse. The unstructured data warehouse is defined and benefits are given. There are several features of the conventional data warehouse that can be leveraged for the unstructured data warehouse, including ETL processing, textual integration, and iterative development.

Chapter 4 focuses on the heart of the unstructured data warehouse: Textual Extract, Transform, and Load (ETL). This chapter has separate sections on extracting text, transforming text, and loading text. The chapter emphasizes the issues around source data. There are a wide variety of sources, and each of the sources has its own set of considerations. Extracting pointers are provided, such as reading documents only once and recognizing common and different file types. Transforming text requires addressing many considerations discussed in this chapter, including phrase recognition, stop word filtering, and synonym replacement. Loading text is the final step. There are important points to understand here, too, that are explained in this chapter, such as the importance of the thematic approach and knowing how to handle large volumes of data. Two ETL examples are provided, one on email and one on spreadsheets.

Chapter 5 describes the 11 steps required to develop the unstructured data warehouse. The methodology explained in this chapter is a combination of both traditional system development lifecycle and spiral approaches.

Unstructured data, of which textual data is a prominent part, is data whose content and organization appear in an irregular and unpredictable manner. There are many forms of unstructured data. Unstructured data is found in text, images, television, the Internet, movies, x-rays, and many, many more places. Colors, images, sounds, shapes, and the like are unquestionably forms of unstructured data. Yet most of the technology to capture, store, and manage unstructured data is immature. Indeed, the technology for the handling of textual data is far more advanced than the technology for handling most other forms of unstructured data. Therefore, for the purposes of this book, when we refer to unstructured data we refer to text.

Text comes in many forms and shapes. Saying that all text is the same is like saying that all humans are the same. While it is true that humans share common traits such as noses, hands, DNA, feet, and other body parts, there are also many differences between humans. Some humans are tall and some are short. Some humans are old and some humans are young. Some humans are black and some humans are white. Some humans are men and some humans are women. There are many differences between humans, even though humans share common characteristics. Text traditionally exists in four different forms: documents, email, spreadsheets, and embedded text. See Figure 1.1.

Figure 1.1 Different forms of text

Documents

...This agreement constitutes the complete understanding of the parties. This Agreement may not be modified or altered except by written instrument executed by the Authors and the Publisher. No waiver of any term or condition of this Agreement or of any breach of this Agreement or of any part thereof, shall be deemed a waiver of any other term or condition of this Agreement or of any later breach of the Agreement or of any part thereof.

Email

```
John, want to do
dinner this
Friday?
Would be great to
catch up.
Let me know -
thanks!


Martin
```

Spreadsheets

	Region A	Region B	Region C	Region D
January	$ 44.00	$ 63.00	$ 32.00	$ 41.00
February	$ 21.00	$ 1.00	$ 74.00	$ 84.00
March	$ 66.00	$ 213.00	$ 216.00	$ 945.00
April	$ 216.00	$ 8.00	$ 7.00	$ 219.00
May	$ 5.00	$ 90.00	$ 94.00	$ 4.00
June	$ 5.00	$ 67.00	$ 105.00	$ 52.00

Embedded text

Coupons

If you have a coupon or promotional code you may enter it here.

Coupon Code:

DXB1932

APPLY COUPON

Special Instructions

Please ship the books as soon as possible as I need them for a presentation next week. The books should be packaged accordingly to prevent them from getting wet from the rain which is in the forecast the next few days.

In addition, text can be described in five different ways: homogeneity, relevance, medium, volume, and structure. Table 1.1 contains the template showing the relationship between form and characteristic.

Table 1.1 Text forms and characteristics

		Form			
		Documents	Email	Spreadsheets	Embedded text
Characteristics	Homogeneity	mixed	homogeneous	homogeneous	mixed
	Format	depends	depends	depends	depends
	Medium	mixed	electronic	electronic	electronic
	Volume	varied	usually large	varied	varied
	Structure	very mixed	very consistent	very consistent	usually consistent

The remainder of this chapter will discuss Table 1.1 in more detail.

Text Form

Text can exist as documents, email, spreadsheets or embedded text.

DOCUMENTS

The normal place in which text is found is documents. It is documents that hold medical records, birth certificates, loans, articles, research, and a thousand other forms. Documents, then, are the basic structure in which text is placed.

EMAIL

One important type of unstructured data is the email. The email is common and is a part of everyday life in most modern parts of the world. Emails have certain characteristics:

- There are no rules as to what the content of an email may be (you can write anything that you want in an email)
- Most (but not all) emails are short

- Many emails are personal and have little or nothing to do with business or commerce.

In addition, emails can contain attachments. In those attachments, oftentimes, there are many useful and interesting items of information. In truth, from a business perspective, the attachments are usually more interesting than the emails themselves.

SPREADSHEETS

Another ubiquitous form of unstructured data is the spreadsheet. Spreadsheets are everywhere. Spreadsheets are the ultimate in personally controlled and personally managed data. There is much pithy information that can be found on spreadsheets, but there are some limitations that you need to be aware of. The first problem is that a cell of data in a spreadsheet is entirely dependent on the spreadsheet for its context and meaning. Looking at a cell and nothing but the cell tells you almost nothing. In order to understand what a cell means, you need to understand what the column in the spreadsheet represents and, for calculated data, the formula behind the cell.

A second limitation of a spreadsheet is that, for the most part, spreadsheets are completely dependent on the individual building and using the spreadsheet. From a format standpoint, it is a good bet that any one spreadsheet is unlike any other spreadsheet in an organization. When trying to read and interpret textual data from a spreadsheet, this individuality factor must be taken into account.

Nevertheless, there often is textual data on a spreadsheet that would be quite useful to include in the corporate unstructured data warehouse.

EMBEDDED TEXT

Another form of text that is a foundation from which the unstructured data warehouse is built is embedded text. Occasionally, in the middle of a very structured file, there is what is commonly termed a "comments" field. It is in the comments field that an engineer, a customer, or a clerk, can insert free form comments. These comments, which are in text form, often contain very valuable information. Comment fields are a very legitimate source of information for the analyst who wishes to build the unstructured data warehouse.

Text Characteristics

Text can be described in terms of homogeneity, format, medium, volume, and structure. Each of these factors shapes how the unstructured data warehouse will be built and used.

HOMOGENEITY

The homogeneity of a document refers to the way that the document is similar to another document in terms of text formats. Text formats can be homogenous, semi-homogeneous, and non-homogeneous. A resume is homogeneous to another resume. A novel is semi-homogenous to a textbook. A contract is non homogenous to an x-ray.

For example, the content of articles is notoriously non-homogeneous. For example, consider the following publications: the National Enquirer, The New York Times, Playboy magazine, and Architectural Digest. It is likely that articles from these publications have few similarities among them. The language, the terms, the subjects discussed, the style of writing, are usually very dissimilar. When addressing very dissimilar documents, the best that can be done is to dissect the documents and cross reference the different text found in them so that the person using the data warehouse that is created has the best chance of finding whatever he/she is looking for.

Now consider patents. Patents, in general, have similar structures because of the application process that all patents go through. Now consider patents dealing with drugs; the patents would have a certain similarity, both in structure and in content, but the terminology would not be exactly the same across all of the patents and the specifics about each drug would vary considerably from one patent to the next. These are semi-homogeneous documents.

Now consider contracts. Say that there are 50 or so oil and gas lease contracts. The contracts are very, very similar. Indeed, there are some differences between one contract and the next, but all in all, there are major areas of the contract that are exactly the same — from one contract to the next. These contracts would be a case of homogeneous documents. By having contracts that are very similar, the analyst can look for common types of data across the different contracts. The analyst can look for and recognize such things as contract date, lessor, lessee, acreage, and so forth.

FORMAT

Format describes the importance of one format of text to another. The actual format of a document plays a part in determining its usefulness and understandability. A novel will most likely not have much relevance to a medical report, whether the report contains properly formed sentences or not. A doctor's report contains very few sentences, whereas a report to the SEC contains finely crafted sentences.

On occasion, a document is divided up into a cell structure (like a spreadsheet). An Excel spreadsheet has its own internal structure, whereas a textbook has a very loose internal structure. A lab report contains results. Occasionally, a result warrants an explanation, regardless of whether the document resides on paper or is in an electronic format.

MEDIUM

The medium for most text of interest in today's world is electronic. Yet there is still a significant amount of text that only exists in a written or printed form on paper.

VOLUME

The volume of unstructured text refers to both the number of documents to be managed and the size of the documents, individually and collectively. An organization may have many small documents, such as email, or many large documents, such as books, patents, or reports. Or an organization may have only a few small or large documents. Considering that most organizations have a variety of documents they might want to include in their unstructured data warehouse, there is likely to be a mixture of large and small documents, with the number of documents varying by the type or subject matter of the documents.

The volume of data within the document and the number of documents are also considerations to the analyst who will build the unstructured data warehouse. See Figure 1.2.

Figure 1.2 Different types of documents

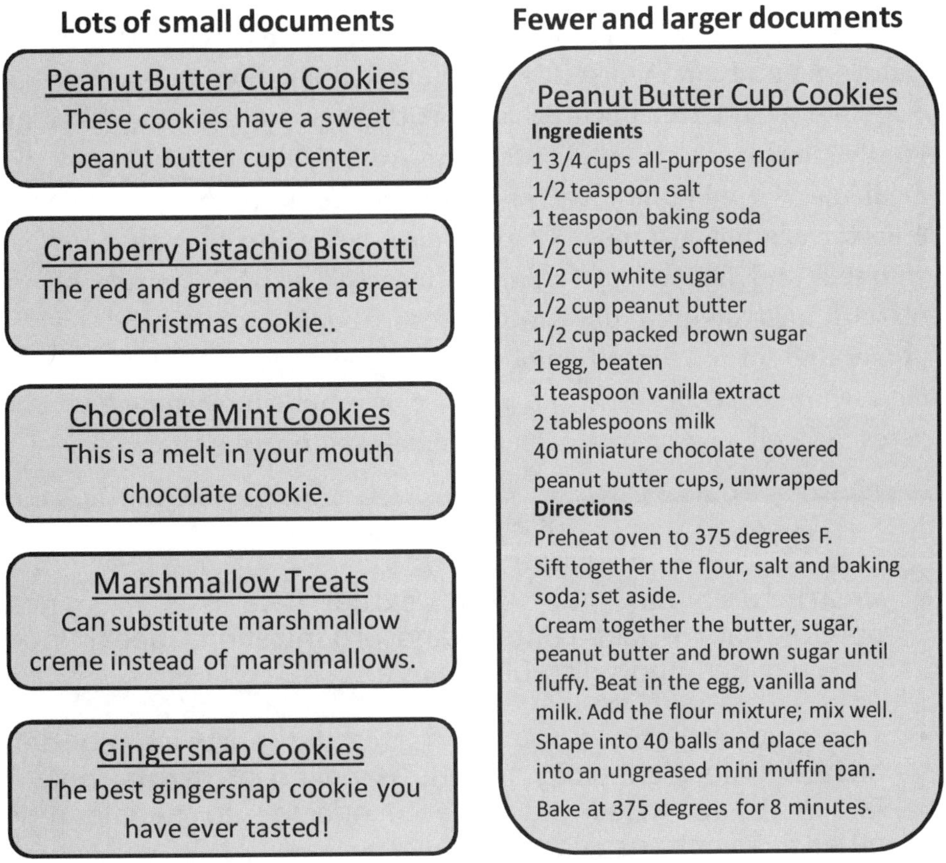

Lots of small documents

Peanut Butter Cup Cookies
These cookies have a sweet peanut butter cup center.

Cranberry Pistachio Biscotti
The red and green make a great Christmas cookie..

Chocolate Mint Cookies
This is a melt in your mouth chocolate cookie.

Marshmallow Treats
Can substitute marshmallow creme instead of marshmallows.

Gingersnap Cookies
The best gingersnap cookie you have ever tasted!

Fewer and larger documents

Peanut Butter Cup Cookies
Ingredients
1 3/4 cups all-purpose flour
1/2 teaspoon salt
1 teaspoon baking soda
1/2 cup butter, softened
1/2 cup white sugar
1/2 cup peanut butter
1/2 cup packed brown sugar
1 egg, beaten
1 teaspoon vanilla extract
2 tablespoons milk
40 miniature chocolate covered peanut butter cups, unwrapped
Directions
Preheat oven to 375 degrees F.
Sift together the flour, salt and baking soda; set aside.
Cream together the butter, sugar, peanut butter and brown sugar until fluffy. Beat in the egg, vanilla and milk. Add the flour mixture; mix well. Shape into 40 balls and place each into an ungreased mini muffin pan.
Bake at 375 degrees for 8 minutes.

STRUCTURE

Structure has two contexts. First is whether or not the document contains its own internal structure. Examples of structured documents include the Bible, which has chapters and verses, a recipe book, with its different recipes, and an atlas, with different maps and sections. The logical sections of a document make a big difference in how the words in the document are to be treated and interpreted.

When a document has important logical subdivisions, the document is referred to as "semi-structured". Documents without an internal structure are more free form, such as letters, notes, and comments.

Another way to look at structure is to consider the structure of the content of the text. Some text is in perfectly formed English sentences; there are verbs, nouns, pronouns, and adjectives. There is proper spelling and there is punctuation. Typically, books and articles are of this variety of text. But very important text exists in other formats, as well. For example, doctors take notes in the form of shorthand and comments; it is very unusual for them to take notes in complete, well-formed sentences. Yet the notes the doctor takes are vitally important to understanding much about healthcare and medicine. Stated differently, just because the notes that are taken by a doctor are not in proper English does not mean that they are not valuable and important. It simply means that the creation of any textual unstructured data warehouse should not depend on the proper and formal formation of text into sentences. The unstructured data warehouse needs to be able to accommodate comments and notes, as well as properly formed English sentences.

Key Points

- Unstructured data, of which textual data is a prominent part, is data whose content and organization appear in an irregular and unpredictable manner.

- The focus of this book is on textual unstructured data because the technology for the handling of textual data is far more advanced than the technology to handle most other forms of unstructured data.

- Text traditionally exists in four different formats: documents, email, spreadsheets, and embedded text.

- Text can be described in five different ways: homogeneity, format, medium, volume, and structure.

This chapter will point out the challenges in accessing and making meaningful data from the unstructured environment. It is entirely possible to query raw unstructured data in much the same way that search engines search, but as you will see in this chapter, merely searching unstructured data is not the same thing as analyzing unstructured data. In order to be effective, the analyst must address the many different issues of unstructured data before a search and analysis can be meaningful. So exactly how can unstructured data be effectively analyzed? The approach described in this book bridges the gap between the structured and the unstructured world. Building a well thought out and meaningful bridge between the two worlds in an unstructured data warehouse opens up a whole new set of analysis and business opportunities. This bridge can be crossed after understanding and addressing the challenges of volume, blather, the Tower of Babel, spelling, lack of natural relationships, data junkyards, and storage format.

Volume

The first major challenge to reducing unstructured data into a usable and analyzable form is the problem of the volume of unstructured data that accumulates. Organizations decide to hold emails for a long period of time. They hold contracts well past their expiration date and medical records for years and years. For a variety of legal and technical reasons, organizations hold unstructured data for a long time.

Unstructured data, itself, is inherently bulky to begin with, but when unstructured data is held for a lengthy amount of time, the sheer volume of data increases dramatically. There are many studies that reveal the existing large volume of unstructured data in many of our organizations, as well as the alarming growth rate of unstructured data. Some surveys predict that unstructured data volume will increase at over a 60% compounded annual growth rate!

It is one thing to try to swim the English Channel. All things considered, the English Channel is a relatively small body of water, sitting snugly between England and France. But swimming from San Francisco to Hawaii is another matter, altogether. It is simply too far to even contemplate an attempt. The volume of water that must be negotiated between France and England is doable. But when that volume is magnified, any attempt to negotiate the water is not even thinkable.

Similarly, searching and managing a modest amount of unstructured data is a challenge, but a challenge that can be met. But when there is an overwhelming amount of data in the unstructured environment, even simple, everyday operations become circumspect. Specifically, a large volume of data can:

- **Add to the costs of storing unstructured data**. As the volume of data increases, not only are more storage costs incurred, but more infrastructure is required, such as processors, software, and connectivity.
- **Make finding useful unstructured data unnecessarily complicated**. One way of thinking about the effect of massive amounts of unstructured data is that useful data hides behind non useful data. For example, consider a lawyer who works with case law. There may be one or two cases that are useful for the issues at hand, but those one or two cases are hidden among tens of thousands of cases that are not useful. To find the useful cases, the lawyer has to have some way of wandering through or getting past all the non useful cases.
- **Make everyday operations cumbersome and awkward**. In a world of large volumes of data, simple activities such as adding indexes and loading data become painful. This, of course, is the same phenomenon that has been noted with standard structured data warehouse processing.

Blather

Another challenge of massive amounts of unstructured data is that of storing data that is not relevant to the business. Since there are no rules for the creation of unstructured data, it stands to reason that some unstructured data is simply not relevant to the business. When a man writes an email to his spouse, "Honey, let's go out for dinner tonight, I had a hard day at the office", this email would not normally be considered relevant to any business. Emails such as these get in the way of the important emails whose content contains information about the business of the organization.

The term that is applied to these non relevant emails is "blather". Blather is the unstructured information that exists in the organization's store of unstructured data that is not relevant to the business of the organization. Blather is a serious problem that must be addressed when building an unstructured data warehouse.

Blather exists in many places other than email. Consider a technical manual - when a technician is searching through the manual, there is likely to be much more information that is not relevant or useful to the problem that needs to be solved than there is data that is useful. Or consider a patent application. From an intellectual property standpoint, the only really important part of the patent is the claims section; everything else is window dressing.

Blather, of course, is in the eye of the beholder. What is blather to one person may not be blather at all to another person. In building the unstructured data warehouse, the analyst must determine what is and is not blather to the majority of the users of the data warehouse.

How much blather a corporation has relative to the total amount of unstructured data is anyone's guess. Depending on the organization, the amount of unstructured data that has been stored, the type of unstructured data that has been stored, the length of time that unstructured data has been stored, and other factors, the percentage of blather will vary widely. But however much or little blather there is, it is a problem when making a serious attempt to come to grips with the processing of unstructured data. Blather needs to be removed entirely, or at least minimized, before effective unstructured processing can begin.

The Tower of Babel

The "Tower of Babel" issue is perhaps the largest and most complex issue to deal with when facing unstructured data. In the Bible, we are told that long ago the peoples of the earth gathered together in order to build a tower up to heaven. The construction project failed because the peoples of the earth spoke different languages and could not coordinate their construction efforts. Thus, the importance of language integration was established long before there ever was a computer.

The Tower of Babel challenge refers to the fact that merely collecting unstructured data is not enough to start to analyze unstructured data. A great deal of attention will be placed on the resolution of this problem of language integration when we discuss obtaining and integrating unstructured data, later in this text. When unstructured data is collected it is a very good bet that the data is logically inconsistent. Logical inconsistency refers to the fact that in one document a word means one thing and in another document the same word means something entirely different. Take unstructured medical data as an example.

In Figure 2.1, it is seen that a search is made on medical terms. The term "ha" appears frequently. The analyst is curious as to the meaning of the term "ha". The analyst discovers that when doctors are writing, the term "ha" is quite common. When a cardiologist writes "ha", the meaning is heart attack. When an endocrinologist writes "ha", the meaning is Hepatitis A. When a general practitioner writes "ha", the meaning is headache. In order to create a firm foundation for query and analytical processing, the term "ha" must be spelled out into its fuller meaning. Otherwise patients with very different afflictions will be grouped together.

Figure 2.1 Tower of Babel example

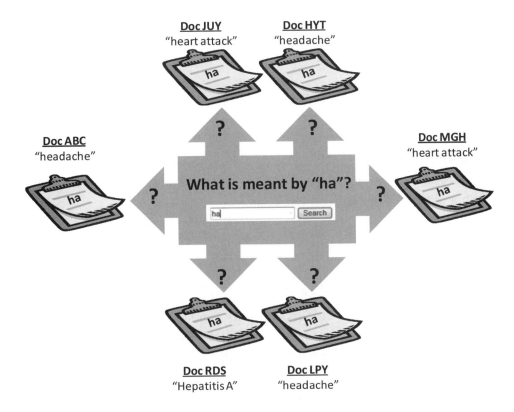

Everyone is focused on the same problem: health; but everyone is speaking a different dialect. It is a classic Tower of Babel problem. Lots of workers are trying to solve the same problem, but all speaking a different language.

In order to make an analysis of unstructured data meaningful, the unstructured data needs to be integrated. Otherwise, the queries executed against the unstructured data will produce results that are heavily and negatively influenced by the different dialects and different languages that are contributing to the collection of unstructured data from many and diverse sources.

Spelling

When working with text, there are other problems, such as alternate forms of the same text. For example, some people have many ways to spell their name. Bill Inmon has several alternate spellings including:

- Billy Inmon
- William Inmon
- Will Inmon
- Willie Inmon
- W H Inmon

If a search is made on the literal "Bill Inmon", it will turn up only occurrences of the exact term. What will be missed are the alternate forms of the name "Bill Inmon".

Looking for the words literally does not produce a hit where the name is spelled differently. When data is integrated, the different spellings of names are also incorporated into the integrated data. So when a search is done on all the alternative names that Bill Inmon is known by, a very different set of results appears. In order to properly prepare unstructured data for effective query processing, it is necessary to take into account alternate spellings and forms of names and words.

Lack of Natural Relationships

One of the foundations of the structured data warehouse is the design of data based on normalization. Normalization is the way that data is organized into a database based on relational theory. When a structure is normalized, all of the elements of the structure fit "naturally" in the grouping, and not into some other grouping of data. For a detailed explanation of normalization, refer to the works done by Chris Date and Ted Codd. For a less formal yet thorough explanation of normalization, refer to **Data Modeling Made Simple** by Steve Hoberman. Normalization has long been one of the backbones of relational theory. With normalization, database design is based on the "natural" relationships that exist among data elements. The founders of normalization theory noted that certain elements of data "belonged" to other elements of data based on existence criteria. Using existence criteria, the data elements were then structured into tables.

Once normalization was applied to database design, the result was a way to create many tables of data, each table having a few elements of related data. The tables taken collectively produced a very granular and flexible design. Normalization has several different degrees or "forms". Third normal form is the basis, or at least the starting point for most database designs found in the structured environment.

Database design for the unstructured environment is very different. With unstructured data, there is no "natural" relationship of one word or phrase to the next. The only relationship between words/phrases in an unstructured document is that they exist in the same document. For example, the phrases "Sarbanes Oxley, revenue recognition, promise to deliver, contingency sale" and "Human resources, salary, date of birth, education, stock options" have no natural relationships between them. For that reason, the notion of normalization is foreign to the world of unstructured data. Therefore, we cannot take advantage of the formal process of normalization for adding flexibility and integrity to our designs based purely upon the raw unstructured data.

Storage Format

Although normalization is foreign to the world of unstructured data, the output of the textual integration of unstructured data can be stored in a relational format. Note that being placed in a relational format does not mean being placed in a rich file format or a blob format. The relational format holds unstructured text quite nicely after the text has been integrated.

There are actually many different ways to create the relational structure. Perhaps the easiest way is to create tables based on the text found in documents.

There is a real advantage to placing unstructured data in a relational, flat file environment. Once text is integrated and placed into a flat file relational format, the integrated unstructured data is able to be accessed and analyzed by standard BI (business intelligence) tools and software.

Data Junkyards

One of the foundations of organizing unstructured data is that of the integration of unstructured data. Data integration is the planned and controlled transformation and flow of data across databases, for operational and/or analytical use.[1] Simply trying to create a foundation of unstructured data out of raw, unintegrated, unstructured data does not produce a data warehouse, it produces a data junkyard. Because text is non repetitive and free form, there is no basic organization to it unless the text has been processed (that is, integrated). Just throwing text into a database without going through a disciplined and well-organized process produces nothing useful. Integration of unstructured data is absolutely mandatory if the query and analytic process that will access the data is to be meaningful. Unstructured raw data must be integrated before the query process can be meaningful. Without integration, analysis of text is meaningless for a hundred reasons. Of course textual integration takes many different forms, most of which are covered subsequently in this book.

So why exactly is integration of unstructured data so important? The following examples will illustrate some of the reasons why integration of unstructured data is so vital.

Consider a simple query made against unstructured data about a "broken bone". Figure 2.2 shows this simple query made against raw unstructured data and against integrated unstructured data.

---

[1] The DAMA Dictionary of Data Management, Technics Publications, LLC, 2008.

Figure 2.2 Data Junkyard example

Where is the information about a "broken bone"?

| broken bone | Search |

Unintegrated data yields only direct hits, yet integrated
unstructured data brings back a more complete set of document

Returned when unintegrated?	Documents	Returned when integrated?
Yes	Doc ABC contains "broken bone"	Yes
No	Doc JUY contains "fractured scaffiod"	Yes
No	Doc HYT contains "cast types"	Yes
No	Doc RDS contains "ruptured disk"	Yes
No	Doc LPY contains "compound fracture"	Yes
No	Doc JUY contains "osteogenesis imperfecta"	Yes

When the query is run against raw unstructured data, the query
yields results where the term "broken bone" is literally found; a few
hits are made. Now consider the results when the same query is run
against integrated unstructured data. The results are not just where
the term "broken bone" is found, but also includes hits of information
closely related to a broken bone. The hit may be on an alternate form
of the term broken bone, or on a term, word, or phrase that is closely
related to a broken bone. Because the data is integrated and the
terms that are similar or related to broken bone have been
determined, the same query yields dramatically more robust results.

The ability to relate terms in the process of integration greatly enhances the unstructured data. When faced with the Tower of Babel proposition (which almost every analyst must face), the ability to relate words and terms as one of the processes of integration is extremely valuable. As explained earlier, if language itself becomes a barrier to communication, then there is little or no chance for a positive result to be achieved by more than one party. But addressing the issues of language integration associated with the Tower of Babel is not the only issue addressed by integration of unstructured data.

There are many good reasons why placing integrated unstructured data in a relational format, then allowing the unstructured data to be accessed and analyzed by standard Business Intelligence (BI) tools is a good idea. Some of those reasons are:

- The standard BI environment contains many ways to analyze data
- In many organizations, the standard BI environment is already in place and paid for
- Many business users have already been trained in the use of the standard BI environment
- With the standard BI environment, queries can be made on data from the structured environment and the unstructured environment at the same time.

Paper

In most cases, modern organizations have the majority of their text in an electronic format. But occasionally text resides on paper. There are some serious disadvantages of having text stored on paper. One is that over time paper deteriorates. Another is that paper takes up a lot of space. A third is that when paper is used up, it must be discarded. A fourth is that paper is highly flammable. A fifth is that doing a manual search of paper is very, very labor intensive. Nevertheless, paper is the medium on which much text starts life.

Trying to do textual integration on paper or between paper and electronic documents faces some serious obstacles. There are several technologies that are useful for bringing text off of paper and into an electronic medium. Each of the technologies has their advantages and disadvantages.

Key Points

- Useful unstructured data hides behind unuseful unstructured data.

- Blather is the unstructured information that exists in the organization's store of unstructured data that is not relevant to the business of the organization.

- The Tower of Babel challenge refers to the fact that merely collecting unstructured data is not enough to start analyzing unstructured data.

- Just collecting unstructured data and doing nothing with it to make it usable leads to a Data Junkyard.

- With unstructured data, there is no "natural" relationship of one word to the next. The only relationship between words in an unstructured document is that they exist in the same document. For that reason the notion of normalization is foreign to the world of unstructured data.

- The best format the unstructured data can be placed in is a relational format so that the integrated unstructured data is able to be accessed and analyzed by standard BI tools and software.

CHAPTER 3

Evolving to the Unstructured Data Warehouse

Today's world of information processing is dominated by database management systems, online transactions, queries, and reports. Tomorrow's world will be dominated by information found in text. To date, text has not been handled well (or at all!) by standard technology. Standard technology is geared for handling repetitive data – data that occurs over and over in the same form and structure. Textual data is decidedly not repetitive and does not fit comfortably with standard technology. But there is a wealth of information in textual data. This chapter will tell you about what needs to be done to fit text within the context and confines of standard technology. In doing so, an entirely new world of decision-making becomes possible. Information that heretofore has never been used in decision making is now open to the organization. This chapter begins with a timeline of applications, highlighting their evolution over the decades, right up through the DW 2.0 architecture, which leads into the role of the unstructured data warehouse. There are several features of the conventional data warehouse that can be leveraged for the unstructured data warehouse, including ETL processing, textual integration, and iterative development.

We Have Come a Long Way

As the cartoon from the prior page illustrates, in the beginning there was paper tape and punched cards. There is no question that data stored on paper tape and punched cards was an improvement over data that was stored on paper and pencil and hands and fingers. Soon, paper tape and punched cards gave way to magnetic tape. With magnetic tape, much more data could be stored, and a magnetic tape did not spill its contents in disarray over the floor when dropped, as did punched cards. But magnetic tape had its limitations, too, and soon there was disk storage. With disk storage, data could be accessed directly and quickly. In short order, disk storage replaced most of the uses of magnetic tape.

The applications that were built using early technology tended to be applications that were somewhat incidental to the running of the business. Early applications included such functional areas as batch oriented accounts payable, accounts receivable, payroll, and so forth. While these applications were certainly important, if there were problems, the day to day business did not stop.

The ability to access data directly quickly led to a new class of application: the online application. An online application is one where the end user interacts with the system, doing updates and queries where the interaction is measured in seconds. With online applications, the computer became an integral part of the business. Prior to online applications, the computer was a useful and interesting part of the business landscape, but there were not many "mission critical" applications. Mission critical applications are those that are central to the day to day activities of the organization. When a mission critical application fails, the organization feels the pain of failure immediately. But with the ability to directly access data, a whole new class of applications became a possibility. Soon there were airline reservation systems, bank teller applications, manufacturing work flow applications, and so forth. In rapid order, the computer became an essential part of the business. When the online application went down, the front line operations of the corporation suffered.

So powerful were these new classes of applications that they began to spring up everywhere. Soon there were applications of every sort to be found all over the corporation.

Caught in the Spider's Web

With the proliferation of applications came a new problem: the organization woke up one day and found that it had data everywhere. Unfortunately, that data appeared in more than one place and no one knew what the correct and accurate value of the data really was. One department had a value of $4,000 while another department had a value of $10,000 for the same unit of data. Making proper decisions based on the splintered, unintegrated data that resulted from the proliferation of applications was an exercise in futility. These early system had evolved into a state of architecture that is often called the "spider's web environment"[2] (or "siloed systems").

Making matters worse was the fact that the more that management tried to ignore the effects of spider's web systems, the worse the effects of spider's web systems became. Spider's web systems caused the information systems of the corporation to go into a death spiral. An information systems death spiral takes place when the practices and architecture of building and operating systems is unsustainable over the long haul.

The earlier cartoon shows the progression to spider's web systems. You can see that the poor fellow is completely covered with spider's webs.

---

[2] The spider's web environment was first discussed in the book **Building the Data Warehouse**, Prentice Hall, 1990

For a long time, organizations were in a state of denial. But as time passed and the ravages of spider's web systems became worse, the organization was finally forced to confront the issue of the architectural deterioration of information systems left in the wake of spider's web systems.

Therefore, the organization discovered that they needed a fundamental change in architectures. The organization discovered that they needed to transition to data warehousing. The costs of maintenance, the inability to get information, and the inability to respond to new requirements all led the organization to understand that the spider's web environment was not sustainable. The frustrations of the spider's web environment led the organization to understand that a change in architecture was needed. Any solution other than a complete change in architecture was merely a Band-Aid solution.

Data Warehouse to the Rescue

A data warehouse was a new structuring of data. A data warehouse is a subject-oriented, integrated, non volatile, time variant collection of data in support of management's decisions[3]. The architecture of the data warehouse represented a real and positive path that organizations could take in order to free themselves from the spider's web systems (sometimes called the "silo systems environment"). Prior to data warehousing, there simply was no notion of "corporate data". Everything in the spider's web environment was application data. As data was put into a data warehouse from the spider's web environment, the data passed through an integration process. In passing through an integration process, the data went from application data to "corporate" data, where the data was representative of the entire corporation, not just a single application. With the data warehouse, for the first time there was the possibility of creating and using data that represented the entire corporation.

---

[3] The data warehouse was defined in the book **Building the Data Warehouse**, Prentice Hall, 1990

The advent of data warehousing represented a fundamental change in the architecture of information technology. Prior to the data warehouse architecture, information systems architecture was architecture that was oriented to building and running applications. Applications architecture did not reflect on the entire corporation. But with data warehouse architecture, there was a way to actually look at data across the corporation. In this regard, the movement to the data warehouse architecture was a significant departure from the way systems were built prior to data warehouse. The earlier cartoon shows the progression to the data warehouse.

For most corporations, the shift to the data warehouse represented a positive and progressive step forward. The data warehouse solved many fundamental corporate problems with information that had been associated with spider's web systems:

- **The creation of corporate data**. Data in the warehouse was a single version of the truth. Without the data warehouse, there was no definitive source of corporate information.
- **The ability to get out of the maintenance backlog conundrum**. Prior to data warehousing, organizations did a lot of work that was called "maintenance". In fact, what was called maintenance was going into legacy systems and trying to squeeze corporate data out of legacy data. Trying to do maintenance on older legacy systems was painful because those systems were never designed for such a task.
- **Data integrity and believability of data**. One of the characteristics of spider's web systems was that the same data existed in multiple places. And the problem with that was that there were different data values for the same item of data. No one knew what the "real" value of data was. But with a data warehouse, there was one and only one unit of detailed data in existence. With a data warehouse, there never was a problem in finding what the "real" value of data was.
- **Data accessibility**. If nothing else, a data warehouse is designed to serve the accessibility needs of lots of people at the same time.

Indeed, data warehousing became conventional wisdom in a short amount of time. Soon corporations everywhere were building and using data warehouses.

But over time, organizations began to find that as powerful as data warehouses were, there were still problems with information inside the data warehouse.

The problems with the classical data warehouse were that the basic lifecycle of data within the data warehouse went unnoticed, that the classical data warehouse was made up of repetitive, transaction-based data only, and that metadata was not an integral part of the infrastructure:

- **Usage drops as volume grows**. The first problem that became apparent was that with a data warehouse, over time, it appeared that there was a lifecycle of data within the data warehouse itself. The lifecycle within the data warehouse was a problem because as the age of data changed, the technology needed to manage the data also changed. As long as data was being held in a single structure and in a single form, the need for different approaches to technology became manifest. Over time people discovered that when data was fresh and new, practically everybody used the data. But as data aged in the data warehouse, the likelihood of the access of that data dropped. Data that was three months old was accessed all the time. But data that was five years old was hardly accessed at all. Weekly sales data for the last quarter was accessed frequently, but that same weekly sales data five years later was seldom if at all used. A second manifestation of the data warehouse lifecycle was that over time the volume of data grew. And therein lay a paradox. The larger the data warehouse grew, the lower the percentage of data that was actually used. The growing disuse of data within the data warehouse is a problem for many reasons – the most obvious is that an organization continues to pay money for storage that is not being used.

- **Limited to primarily repetitive transactions**. The second limitation that was noticed was that data warehouses were built entirely on the basis of classical repetitive transaction-based data. The same activity or business transaction occurred over and over, and each iteration of activity caused a new record of data to be placed in the data warehouse. A banking transaction was done. An airline reservation was made. An insurance claim was processed. Each of these repetitive business activities caused a new record to be written into the data warehouse. The problem was that there were all sorts of important data that were not in the form of a transaction. For example, there was textual unstructured data that never found its way inside a data warehouse. And since businesses relied on data warehouses for decision making, and because non repetitive data was not part of the data warehouse, decisions were made only on the basis of business transactions.

- **Severely lacking metadata**. Yet a third problem was that first generation data warehouses did not contain in any organized manner, metadata. Metadata is the descriptive data about the "mainline" data that exists in a database. Metadata tells you what data is where and how much of that data there is. There was metadata associated with first generation data warehouses. The problem was that the metadata had no formal structure within the structure of the first generation data warehouse. And yet metadata was a very important aspect of the world of analytical processing. It is through metadata that the analyst finds out what data is available for analysis. And there are a hundred other reasons why metadata plays an important role in the world of business intelligence and data warehouse.

Data Warehouse 2.0 to the Rescue

The limitations of first generation data warehouses led to the next architectural evolution – that of the evolution to DW 2.0. DW 2.0 is the architecture of data warehousing and business intelligence that has evolved from first generation data warehouses.[4]

There are several interesting aspects of DW 2.0. The one that is of interest in this book is that of the ability to put unstructured data into a data warehouse. Indeed, the data warehouse that is created by making the contents of the data warehouse from unstructured textual data can be called the unstructured data warehouse.

While the notion of an unstructured data warehouse is new, the architecture in which an unstructured data warehouse fits is not new at all. The genesis of the architecture that the unstructured data warehouse fits into goes back to the corporate information factory (CIF). The corporate information factory grew up around the data warehouse. From the corporate information factory the architectural evolution continued into DW 2.0, put forth by Bill Inmon in 2006. DW 2.0 incorporates many features from its predecessor, the corporate information factory, but the DW 2.0 architecture is notable for several features:

- **The recognition of the lifecycle of data that is apparent inside the data warehouse**. Data is entered, is integrated, is used for analysis, and then is archived. These different stages of the lifecycle of data require different treatment and technology. To try to treat a data warehouse as if it had only one lifecycle while inside the data warehouse is a mistake. For example, when data is first put into a data warehouse, all data is pretty much accessed with the same probability. But as data in the warehouse ages, the probability of access changes dramatically. The newer data has a very high

---

[4] DW 2.0 is described in the book **DW 2.0 – Architecture for the Next Generation of Data Warehousing,** Morgan Kaufmann, 2008. It is also fully described in the web site www.inmoncif.com under DW 2.0.

probability of access. The older data has an increasingly lower probability of access.

- **The recognition that unstructured data belongs in a data warehouse beside structured data**. In the first generation of data warehouses, there was only structured data.

- **The recognition that metadata belongs as an integral part of a data warehouse**. In the first generation of data warehouses, metadata was an afterthought, at best. In DW 2.0, metadata is an integral part of the architecture. In addition, different levels of metadata are recognized. There is local metadata and global metadata. Local metadata is that metadata that is relevant to and applicable to only one component of the architecture. Global metadata is that metadata that is applicable to the entire architecture.

There are many other features of DW 2.0 that represent the next generation beyond first generation data warehouses. It may not be clear how an unstructured data warehouse fits with DW 2.0. In fact, DW 2.0 is divided into different components. The three major components of the DW 2.0 architecture are the unstructured component, the structured component, and the metadata component. Figure 3.1 shows these different components.

Figure 3.1 Components of the DW 2.0 environment

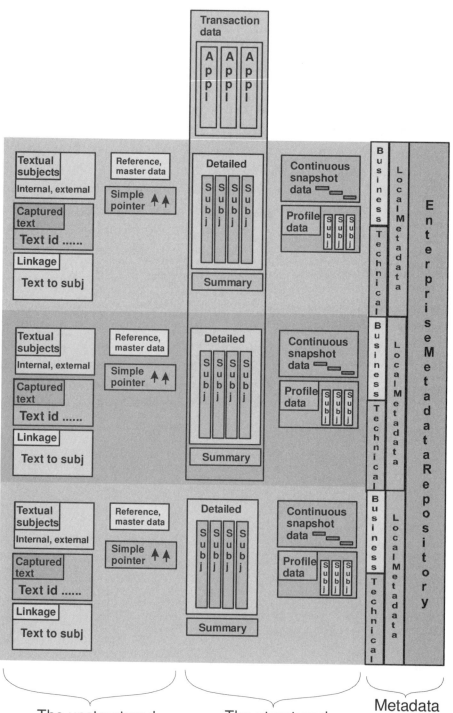

UNSTRUCTURED COMPONENTS

There are many different unstructured components that are specified by DW 2.0. In one form or another, these components from DW 2.0 can be placed or built in the unstructured data warehouse. Some of the important components include:

- **Simple pointer data**. A simple pointer is where an unstructured word or phrase has its reference to the source text disclosed. As an example, the word "hathaway" is found in doc "rty", word "12998".
- **Textual subjects**. This includes both external and internal subjects. As an example, the words in the doc "yut" all center around liver cancer.
- **Captured text**. This includes where the actual text is brought over from the unstructured environment. For example, email "bnn1226" says "let's embezzle some more money."
- **Linkage**. This is the linkage from unstructured to structured data. As an example, the email address binmon@inmondatasystems.com is linked to the customer known as "bill inmon" so that any email with that 'from' email address can be identified as coming from him.
- **Reference data**. This is where reference tables are stored. For example, it is seen that on "Oct 22, 2006", the term "GM" means "General Mills".

Unstructured Data Warehouse to the Rescue

The history of data warehousing has all been about structured, repetitive, transaction-based data. That was yesterday. But when we look at the future data warehouse, we see the advent of unstructured textual data.

In most organizations there are two types of systems: unstructured and structured systems. Structured systems are those whose content is well ordered (that is, predictably ordered and organized). Everything is in neat, well ordered tables and columns. There are indexes. There are structured definitions. There are reports, and so forth. Structured data usually comes from transactions. As business transactions are executed, the data that is a byproduct of the transaction is gathered. Once the customer behavior pattern is understood, the arrival of transactions and the collection of data becomes a rote exercise. High performance and high availability are trademarks of structured systems. An entire IT industry has grown up servicing the needs of structured processing.

The other type of system that has emerged is the unstructured system. The unstructured environment is one where little or no structured data exists. Everything is freeform in the unstructured environment. When you read a textual based document, there is no predefined or predictable sensibility to the document. The author can write anything that he/she pleases. Not even the rules of grammar or spelling must be followed. When doctors write notes, they do not write in sentences. When teenagers IM (instant message), they do not write in full words or complete sentences. In truth, when someone sits down to write, the result can be anything.

These two environments, structured and unstructured, have grown up side by side. Ironically, there is little or no interaction or interchange of data between these environments. In many ways, it is as if the two environments are ignorant of each other. Data does not flow from the unstructured world to the structured world, and vice versa.

This gulf of indifference takes many forms:

- **Historical**. People have not bridged the gap in the past, so why should they start now. Organizations have run happily and successfully for many years, so why should anything change?
- **Technological**. Technology is designed to operate in one environment or the other, but not both. Transaction processing does not work on text, and email processing does not work well on transactions, for example.
- **Organizational**. An organizational unit is mandated to operate in one environment or the other, but not both. You have a sales organization that relies heavily on conversation

with a prospect or client and you have a shipping department that hardly engages in any conversation at all.

- **Cultural**. People think one way or the other, but not both. People orient themselves to their job, and most jobs do not overlap much between conversation and transaction processing.

There are, then, many reasons why there is a gulf of differences between the two environments. It is truly unfortunate, because there is great opportunity for those organizations that successfully cross the gulf. Crossing the gulf between structured and unstructured data allows organizations to do a class of analytical processing that has never before been possible. And this class of analytical processing has long term and profound business implications. Those organizations that cross the gulf find that there is information to manage the business as never before. For example suppose an organization starts to use the email system in an operational manner (which is a very common occurrence). It may be convenient for day to day operations to use the email system to transact daily activities, but the minute those activities need to be analyzed by management, they are lost because they are in the email system.

The unstructured textual environment is made up of common and readily recognizable technology such as email, medical records, reports, transcripted telephone conversations, documents, and other forms of text. Figure 3.2 shows the common types of technologies that house unstructured textual data.

Figure 3.2 Common types of technologies that house unstructured text

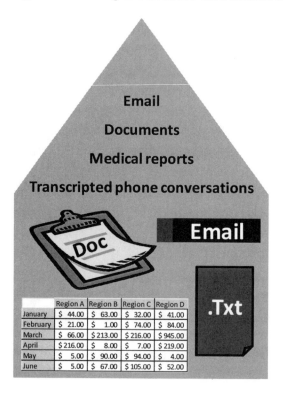

There are some aspects of the unstructured textual environment that at the same time both simplify and add complexity to the process of analysis. Unstructured text is simplified in that it is just language. Everybody uses language. A teenager from Maine and a retiree from Phoenix meet on common ground when examining and analyzing their language. They both speak in sentences, both use words that are reasonably recognizable to the other, and both understand the general idea that the other person is trying to express. The job of the analyst working with text is greatly simplified because whatever the source, it is just language that is being processed. From a technology standpoint, this fact is emancipating. Language can come from the personal computer, from email, from IBM sources, from Sun Microsystems sources, from corporate lawyers, from management, and from clerks. When it comes to unstructured text, it just doesn't matter what the technology is or what the source is. This uniformity of language makes a tremendous difference in simplifying the task of the analyst wishing to analyze text. The analyst using text recognizes and understands the text, whether it is from an order, a memo, a telephone message, television, or a spouse.

At the same time, unstructured text can be perplexing. Unstructured text is incomplete, colloquial, idiosyncratic, and irrelevant much of the time. In a word, just because you can access and gather text easily does not mean that you can use that text analytically. Indeed, as will be seen in this book, unstructured text must be processed in depth in order to be useful.

The most effective way to bridge the gap between the structured and the unstructured world is to build an unstructured data warehouse. An unstructured data warehouse is a collection of integrated text built for analysis. Figure 3.3 depicts an unstructured data warehouse.

Figure 3.3 Unstructured data warehouse

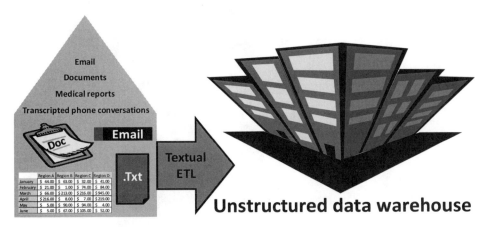

An unstructured data warehouse is one that contains unstructured data that has been integrated and formatted and structured in a manner suitable for analysis. An unstructured data warehouse is one that has all of the characteristics of a classical data warehouse except that the source data flowing into the unstructured data warehouse comes from text and the text has been "integrated", as shall be described. An unstructured data warehouse begins with raw unstructured data. Once collected, the raw unstructured data is then edited, filtered, organized, and consolidated in order to accommodate meaningful unstructured analysis. An unstructured data warehouse is not merely a dumping ground for raw unstructured data.

The first property of an unstructured data warehouse is that it is populated from integrated data flowing from a textual source. Once the unstructured data warehouse has been constructed, it can be analyzed by standard tools of analysis.

But there is another important property of an unstructured data warehouse. That property is once the unstructured data warehouse has been constructed, it can have some of its data connected or related to data in the structured data warehouse. Figure 3.4 shows this important property.

Figure 3.4 Unstructured and structured data warehouses can be linked

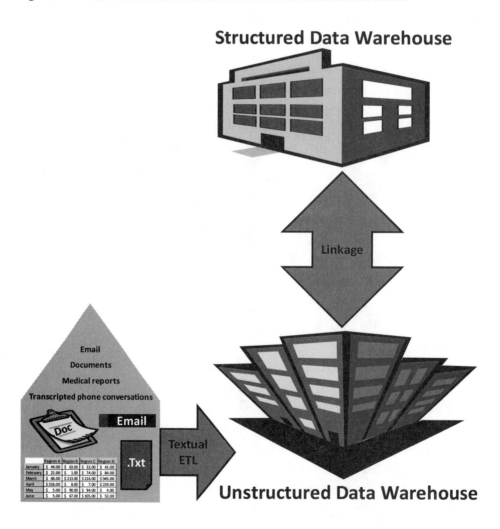

The connection between the unstructured data warehouse and the structured data warehouse is made by means of linkage. Some, but not all data in the unstructured data warehouse has the capability of being linked. When this linkage is made, the result is the possibility for a new and truly important application of a combination of structured and unstructured data.

As a simple example, suppose an organization keeps demographic data about a customer. The source of this demographic data is typically structured data. But suppose emails can be added to the database. Now the organization can keep both demographic data and conversational data about the consumer.

THE THEMATIC APPROACH

There have been attempts in the past to understand unstructured text linguistically. This approach is called the "natural language approach" (or the "NLP" approach).[5] While the linguistic approach has its proponents, the approach that will be described in this book is decidedly non linguistic. The approach followed in this book can best be described as the "thematic" approach to reducing text into an analyzable form and format. The thematic approach is one in which each word is considered to merely be a unit of data in a database. The words can then be organized (that is, clustered) according to themes.

The NLP approach mandates that words and language be understood through the understanding of the context of the words. The linguistic approach is one where the computer is taught the context of language. By understanding the context of language, the actual words that have been spoken can be discerned and understood. In many ways, the linguistic approach mimics the processing that language goes through in the human brain as language is being processed.

The thematic approach mandates that words are simply units of data and are treated accordingly within the confines of the database

---

[5] In order to understand more about the NLP approach, please refer to the Wikipedia entry on NLP

management system that holds the words. The thematic approach is different, in that context of language hardly plays a role. Instead, words are treated as objects. In doing so, a very straightforward processing of words can be achieved.

Because words are treated as objects, there are no boundaries to their usage. For example, in thematic processing, it is fairly easy and not unusual to process different languages. Indeed, it is as easy to process one language as it is to process different languages all at the same time. Figure 3.5 shows that one of the byproducts of thematic processing is the ability to handle multiple languages all at the same time.

Figure 3.5 The thematic approach can be used for many different languages

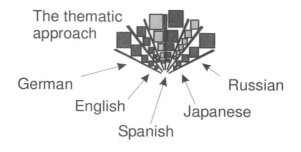

ADVANTAGES OVER A TRADITIONAL SEARCH ENGINE

It is important to understand the difference between a search engine and an unstructured data analytical engine. A search engine is technology that is designed to look for occurrences of text exactly as the text was written. An analytical engine is technology that reads, interprets, and transforms text so that the text can be used for analytical processing. Simply stated, search processing assumes that you cannot make many fundamental changes to text before processing. An analytical engine makes the assumption that many major changes must be made to text before the text is fit for analytical processing. These differences are best illustrated by some examples. Please see Table 3.1.

Table 3.1 Search Engine versus Analytical Engine

Search Engine can do this...	Analytical Engine can do this...
go find all references to Bill Inmon	go find all references to Bill Inmon and the many different spellings of his name
go find references to "ha"	go find references to heart attack, references to headache, and references to hepatitis A where the raw text is "ha"
go find references to Sarbanes Oxley	go find references to all that Sarbanes Oxley is related to, such as "promise to deliver", "contingency sale", "delayed delivery", and "revenue recognition"
go find references to fishing	go find references to fishing in fifteen languages
go find references to "the president"	go find references to "the president" and eliminate all references except those referring to the president of the United States

And there are many, many other examples of the differentiation between search engine processing and unstructured analytical processing.

Leveraging the Traditional Data Warehouse

There are many similarities between the structured and the unstructured data warehouse environments. The data is placed in a relational environment. The data is able to be analyzed using analytical tools. The data can sometimes be linked together. These are important and powerful similarities.

ETL PROCESSING

Another important similarity is in how data finds its way into each of the different environments. Figure 3.6 shows that data is placed into the structured data warehouse environment by means of processing often referred to as ETL processing. ETL stands for "extract/transform and load" technology. ETL has long been used to load a data warehouse from legacy applications. Classical ETL reads legacy data, reformats it, recalculates it, restructures it and does many other activities all designed to turn the data coming from an application into corporate data that fits in a data warehouse.

Figure 3.6 Classical ETL loads into structured data warehouse

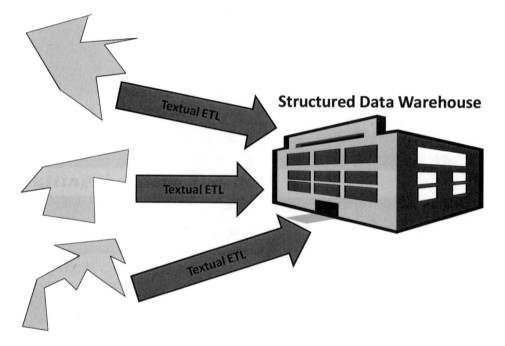

In structured ETL, there are many sources of data, usually older legacy applications. Data is pulled from these older applications, then integrated and placed into a data warehouse. In order for this simple-looking procedure to occur, a lot has to happen. At the very least:

- The target structure of the structured data warehouse must be designed
- The ETL tool must be able to read the technology that the legacy systems are in
- The ETL tool must be able to write the output into the format and technology that has been selected for the structured data warehouse

- The ETL tool must be able to manipulate the data in many ways, including the possible:
  o Summarization of data
  o Editing of data
  o Formatting of data
  o Usage of logic to recast the content of data
  o Addition of time stamps to data
  o Alteration of keys
  o Changing of the physical structure of data
  o Separation of data/aggregation of data.

In brief, the structured ETL process is a detailed, lengthy complex process. Entire careers have been made in the arena of structured ETL. There are many similarities between textual ETL and the ETL traditionally performed in structured data warehouses. These similarities include the following:

- The execution of the processes results in a data warehouse
- Raw data is fed into the process and integrated data results
- Both processes require a special "read" interface, where text is read as a whole entity, not just a disjointed set of words.

However, some of the differences between the processes are:

- One process operates on structured data; the other process operates on unstructured data
- One process is designed to be run repeatedly; the other process is not designed to be run repeatedly
- One process must be aware of the operational window for processing; the other process is not aware of the operational processing window to any great extent
- The logic used to integrate legacy data is very different from the logic needed to integrate unstructured data.

INTEGRATION

The data that is loaded into the unstructured data warehouse has a similar loading process to the process that is used to load data into a structured data warehouse. The process can be called textual integration. Textual integration is the process of reading text and preparing it for analytical processing.

One of the intriguing aspects of textual integration is that of the similarity between textual integration of unstructured data and the integration of legacy data by an ETL tool. Indeed, from a 50,000 foot view, classical legacy ETL and textual integration appear to be identical processes. But the lower the altitude, the more differences there are. Indeed, at 10,000 feet the processes appear to be very different. And once an analyst starts to get into the details of executing the processes, the stark differences between the two processes become apparent.

From a very high level, textual integration is architecturally similar to structured ETL. But the actual workings of textual integration are extremely different from structured ETL processing. Perhaps the biggest difference between structured ETL and textual integration is that in structured ETL, the output of the data warehouse is predetermined. The data warehouse designer is obligated to identify the end results, which is how the structured ETL process knows how to operate. In the case of textual integration, the output is self determining, for the most part. The final result of the unstructured data warehouse is a function of the data found in the input of the unstructured environment. Stated differently, there is essentially no design work that has to be done in order to create an unstructured data warehouse. In the case of textual integration, text is read into the process, and models, categorizations, standard dates, and so forth, are all created.

One of the mysteries of textual ETL is that you have what you have and no amount of design changes anything. This is a 180 degree departure from classical structured ETL. It is hard to see this until you have actually done it. The people that work with me find it second nature now. But when they started it seemed very out of place. Stated differently, when doing unstructured ETL, there is practically no design work that is done, in comparison to the design work done in classical structured ETL.

This means that even though the loading of data in the different environments looks to be the same, in fact it is not. Structured ETL requires a massive and complex effort of design and other preparation. Textual integration merely requires that the processing parameters be set up properly and the final result shapes itself. Textual integration operates under a completely different philosophy than structured ETL. Figure 3.7 contrasts the length of time required to create the different data warehouses.

Figure 3.7 Length of time to create an unstructured vs. structured data warehouse

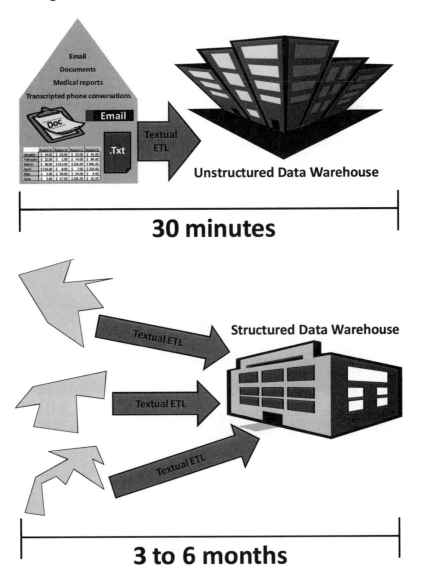

There is another significant difference between structured ETL and textual integration. That difference is in the frequency with which the different processes are applied. Structured ETL is applied as often as there is new transaction data waiting to be processed. This may mean that structured ETL is performed weekly, daily, or even hourly. Textual integration is performed on an as-needed basis. This means that most unstructured data will have to be integrated exactly once in its life. Only if the unstructured data changes, does the textual integration process need to be performed again. This fundamental difference between structured ETL and textual integration is very significant when setting up the day to day operations of these procedures.

ITERATION

The textual integration process for unstructured data is applied in an iterative manner, just as is the structured ETL process. Figure 3.8 shows that textual integration is processed iteratively. First, one pass of integration is made at the text. The results are analyzed, the processing parameters are refined, and the integration processing is repeated on the same text. The refinements that are made are made entirely on the basis of the analysis that is done (or cannot be done) on the data that has been created. If an analysis cannot be done or is done incorrectly, then the parameters that shape the textual data are adjusted so that analysis can be done and can be done correctly. This iterative process continues until the analytical results that are desired are obtained.

Figure 3.8 Iterative development

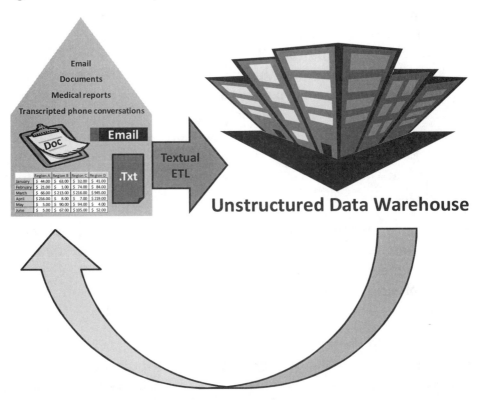

All data warehouses are built iteratively. And this is as true for unstructured data warehouses as it is for any other type of data warehouse. Trying to build a data warehouse in a "big bang" approach, where all data is designed, transformed, and loaded at once is a huge mistake. The big bang approach is a prescription for disaster.

The unstructured data warehouse is built iteratively for lots of good reasons. The primary reason is that the parameters needed to specify what the data warehouse is to look like are almost sure to change. Building an unstructured data warehouse is somewhat like baking a cake. When you bake a cake you mix the ingredients as best you can. But until the cake is baked and out of the oven you really don't know how the cake is going to turn out. If the cake comes out not quite right, you adjust the ingredients and bake another cake, and continue the process until the cake comes out just as you want it.

The unstructured data warehouse is like a cake in that you don't really know how it is going to turn out until it is out of the oven. But there is one significant difference between a cake and an unstructured data warehouse. That difference is that when you bake a cake, the ingredients and the directions for baking the cake are fairly simple and well known. But the ingredients and the mixing of those ingredients for an unstructured data warehouse are very complex and not very well known. Therefore, passing data through textual ETL the first time is sort of like an experiment. It is very unlikely that you are going to get the ingredients just right the first time you do it.

Given that a certain amount of experimentation is necessary when building an unstructured data warehouse, the iterative approach makes imminent sense. If the odds are very good that a certain amount of work is going to have to be redone, then it only makes sense that the work that is done initially be minimized.

The inability to know requirements up front is another good reason why an unstructured data warehouse should be built iteratively. The true requirements for the data warehouse cannot be known until one or two iterations have already been built. When you try to explain to an end user what an unstructured data warehouse is, the end user has a hard time envisioning what you are talking about. But when an end user sees something tangible, then the end user starts to imagine all sorts of requirements. Knowing the real requirements for an unstructured data warehouse is an impossibility until the end user can actually see what is possible.

Key Points

- Spider's web systems led to a fundamental change in architectures. The organization discovered that they needed to transition to data warehousing.

- A data warehouse is a subject oriented, integrated, non volatile, time variant collection of data in support of management's decisions.

- The classic data warehouse had several problems, including usage dropping as volume grew, they were limited to primarily repetitive transactions, and usually these data warehouses lacked metadata.

- DW 2.0 has many interesting aspects, including the ability to put unstructured data into a data warehouse.

- An unstructured data warehouse is one that contains unstructured data that has been integrated and formatted and structured in a manner suitable for analysis. An unstructured data warehouse is one that has all of the characteristics of a classical data warehouse except that the source data flowing into the unstructured data warehouse comes from text and the text has been "integrated".

- ETL processing, textual integration, and iteration are all properties of the existing data warehouse environment that can be leveraged for the unstructured data warehouse environment.

- There are many considerations to the building of the unstructured data warehouse. Some of the considerations are architectural. Some of the considerations are economic. Some of the considerations are technical.

CHAPTER 4
Extracting, Transforming, and Loading Text[6]

At the heart of creating the unstructured data warehouse is the ability to integrate text using Textual Extract, Transform, and Load (ETL). It is by using textual ETL that unstructured text is turned into a database. Stated differently, with textual ETL, raw text goes in and a database that is able to be analyzed and used for decision making comes out. Textual ETL, then, is the technology that exists in order to do textual integration.

Figure 4.1 From raw text to the unstructured data warehouse

---

[6] Much of the material in this chapter is a description of intellectual property which is Patent Pending. If you have a need to use this material in any way – designing a product, refining the design to a product, creating a new product, etc., please contact Forest Rim Technology for licensing information.

Textual ETL has some important similarities and differences with traditional data warehouse ETL, discussed in Chapter 3. The cartoon in Figure 4.1 shows that raw text goes into Textual ETL and that an unstructured data warehouse comes out the other side. This figure shows that the entire objective of integrating text is to support analytical processing against this text. We will refer back to this cartoon throughout this chapter.

There is no great secret in the execution of analytical unstructured data processing. However, there is a groundswell of work that must be done to prepare the data for unstructured analytical processing.

On occasion, it makes sense to split the process of textual integration into two processes. The first process is the reading and preconditioning of the text. The second process is the editing and manipulation of the raw text. Breaking up the process of textual integration into two processes extends the system time to process the text, because two passes through the raw text must be made, rather than one. But there is a tradeoff – much greater flexibility can be achieved in making two passes against the raw text.

For example, suppose you want to index "pit bull". Also suppose that the Textual ETL process can handle only one word. In order to index "pit bull", you have to turn it into one word. The preprocessing can find the words "pit bull" and replace them with "pit_bull". The term "pit_bull" is now treated as one word by the system.

The bulk of the work that must be done for textual integration is work that is done by software specifically designed for the task. The cartoon in Figure 4.1 describes the general structure and shape of a textual integration engine.

Unstructured data is read into the Textual ETL engine. The working components of the Textual ETL engine will be discussed in this chapter and include:

- **A stop words list**. A list of extraneous words such as "a", "and", "the", "was", and "that".
- **A synonym list**. A list of words and phrases that are synonyms.

- **A series of external categories**. A list of the major categorizations of text; a sort of "meta language".
- **A stemming algorithm, such as the Porter algorithm**. An algorithm used to reduce words to their basic stems. Note that stemming can be done with a stemming list rather than by using an interactive algorithm.

Now let's look in detail at each part of the ETL process.

Extracting Text (The 'E' of ETL)

After the general business value of the unstructured data warehouse is established, it is a good idea to look carefully at the source data. Chapter 1 has shown that there are many different forms of unstructured text.

The first step in the integration of unstructured data is that of physically accessing (that is, reading) the unstructured data. Stated differently, if you cannot physically access unstructured data, then you will never be able to integrate the data. Figure 4.2 contains a more detailed version of the textual integration process from Figure 3.3.

Figure 4.2 The 'E' of ETL (Extract)

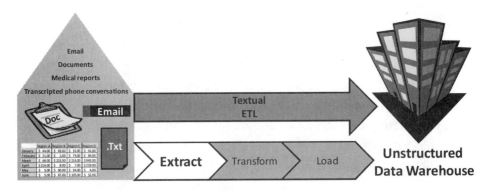

KNOWING THE SOURCE

There are some fairly significant issues in the accessing of unstructured data. The first issue is the source of unstructured data. There are a wide variety of sources and each of the sources has their own set of considerations. Recall the cartoon in Figure 4.1. Common sources of unstructured data include corporate servers and desktops, the Internet, paper, and voice recordings and the resulting transcriptions:

- **Corporate servers and desktops**. Data from the server is read in a compact and efficient manner. Once the reader arrives at the server it is merely a matter of accessing and reading data off the server. Reading data on the desktop is another matter. If the desktop machines are tied together by a network, then in many cases, the data on the desktop can be read by sending a request across the network to each desktop machine. If, however, the desktop machines are not networked together, then each desktop machine must be read individually and the output data must be collected manually.
- **Internet**. There are many ways data can be brought into the unstructured environment from the Internet – by search engines, by crawlers, manually, and so forth.
- **Paper**. Another source of unstructured data is textual information that exists on paper. In order to be processed, paper based textual data must be collected, read, and gathered into an electronic format. Once put into an electronic format, the unstructured data can then be processed. All sorts of documents exist on paper. Contracts, articles, reports, evaluations, income tax filings, and many, many more types of important information exist on paper. As long as these documents only exist on paper, they cannot be usefully accessed, analyzed, or otherwise processed electronically. When the unstructured data is stored on paper, as many, many files are, the paper must be converted into an electronically accessible format. In other words, computers cannot directly read and process text off of paper without going through a conversion from paper to electronic format. One of the common ways that this conversion from paper to electronics is made is through what is termed "OCR", or optical character recognition technology. OCR works fine as long as 100% accuracy of conversion is not required. If the font is regular Times Roman, there is a high accuracy rate of conversion. But the more the font style varies from Times

Roman, the less accurate the conversion rate. Words may become split. The word "manufacture" could turn into the two words, "manu" and "facture". Other words are simply not recognized at all. After OCR is done, a manual effort is required to make the data much more accurate. Unfortunately, this manual cleanup effort is both expensive and time consuming. But there is some good news. Once the cleanup is done (however it is done), it never has to be done again.

- **Transcriptions**. There is another file format that is of note and that file format is transcripted voice recordings, especially telephone calls. Of course, there are legalities that must be considered because it is not legal to capture every telephone conversation, but assuming the legal requirements have been met, captured conversations must then be converted to electronic text. There are numerous software packages which make such transcriptions. The simplest of these merely notes which options have been chosen from a menu. In many ways, these forms of voice transcription are more a form of structured data rather than unstructured data. But other voice recognition software actually attempts to hear words that have been spoken and translate those words into electronic text. As in the case of OCR, the issue then becomes the percentage of accuracy of the conversion. Some of the things that hinder success include regional accents, colloquialisms, garbled speech, incomprehensible pronunciation, chewing gum while talking, and a volume of speech that is too low to be recognizable. There is no such thing as truly achieving 100% accuracy when dealing with voice recognition. However, it should be remembered that the human ear and human understanding is not 100% either. We often do not clearly hear and understand 100% of what is being said. In some cases, we can ask the speaker to repeat what was said. In other cases, the context of what is being said allows our brains to "fill in" the rough spots. And in yet other cases, we simply don't understand what is being said. Therefore, the fact that voice recognition is not 100% accurate should not be a hindrance because human cognition is not

100% either. Before telephone conversations can be used as input, the telephone conversations must be transcripted, and that transcription however it is done, is not an entirely accurate process.

Unstructured data comes in essentially different packages. Some unstructured data is short and voluminous. Emails fit into this category. There are lots of emails but they don't tend to be very long. There are other documents that are very long, but there are relatively few of them. Contracts and medical records may fit into this category. There are other documents whose language is written very formally, and there are others whose content is very informal.

READING DOCUMENTS ONLY ONCE

One of the guiding principles when reading unstructured data is that, once read, the unstructured data should not be read again; unless of course modifications have been made to the unstructured data. Rereading unstructured data when not necessary can be a colossal waste of resources.

There are many good ways to accomplish the objective of reading an unstructured document only once. Perhaps the most common approach is to use the metadata attached to the document to determine when the document was last updated. If there has been an update since the last time the document was considered or processed, then of course the document should be reprocessed. But many documents – once created – are never modified. In fact, with documents such as emails and transcripted telephone calls, later modification may actually be illegal.

Unfortunately, the last modified date is not part of the metadata of some documents. Nevertheless, using last modified date as a basis for reprocessing is a good idea.

IDENTIFYING COMMON FILE TYPES

The reading of unstructured data must encompass data in many types of unstructured files. Some of the common file types that can be used for input into the unstructured integration engine include:

- PowerPoint files - .ppt
- Portable document format files- .pdf
- Text files - .txt
- Document files - .doc
- Excel spreadsheet - .xls
- Email files

In addition to the above common file types that contain unstructured data, there are many file types that can be read as a .txt file.

Many file types have unstructured data as only one component. There are other kinds of data in the file type, as well. PowerPoint files contain a good example of this separation of the file type into different kinds of data. Another example is x-rays, which contain an image component and then the text that goes with the image. Or realtors have home pictures along with the description of the property for sale.

ACQUIRING THE "READ" INTERFACE

In the end, there are three basic ways that software for reading unstructured data can be acquired. Figure 4.3 depicts those three basic sources for reading unstructured data.

Figure 4.3 Sources of software for reading unstructured data

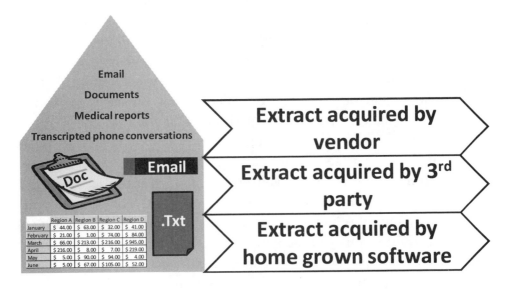

Each source of software for reading unstructured data has its own advantages and disadvantages:

- **Vendor.** When vendor-supplied software is used to read unstructured data, the cost of the software is minimal or is even free. And of course, if the software comes from a vendor, then the software is compatible with other software components supplied by that vendor. Another advantage is that as the software releases change over time, the vendor is responsible for keeping the software they provided up to date with the changes. But there are a surprising set of disadvantages to vendor-supplied software, too. In many cases, the vendor-supplied software is not the best software available. The software supplied by a vendor is often inefficient in execution and is inaccurate. In addition, vendor software is often not reliable. Many vendors advertise their software to be 99% reliable. While 99% reliability may seem to be good enough for most circumstances, it is not what can be termed industrial strength. Industrial strength must be 99.9999999% reliable. While the difference between 99% and 99.9999999% doesn't seem like much, it is when you are reading large volumes of text and in the middle of your 100,000th document the system stops working.

- **3rd party.** Third party software comes from vendors other than the vendor supplying the base DBMS software. The first disadvantage is 3rd party software costs money. But there usually are many advantages to 3rd party software, as well. Usually 3rd party software executes very efficiently. And 3rd party software is highly reliable, as opposed to vendor supplied software. And a final advantage is that the 3rd party is responsible for keeping the software in synch with the different releases of the related software.

- **Home grown.** When you build software interfaces yourself, you can customize them any way you want. They can be made very highly reliable. You can do whatever you want with the interfaces, but you incur the initial cost of creating them. And of course, as software releases change, you are responsible for keeping your own interfaces up to date.

One of the interesting things about unstructured data is that once the unstructured text is gathered, it is unified by being part of a common language (or common languages). Suppose there were 15 different sources of English-based text. A lot of work may have gone into accessing the different sources, but once the text is read from the sources, the text is unified by the language itself. There are verbs, nouns, pronouns, and sentence structure regardless of the original source of the text.

There are, then, different approaches to the creation and maintenance of the interfaces that will be needed to read unstructured data. To illustrate some of the top level considerations of the different forms of raw text, suppose that there is no great similarity from one document to another; or suppose that there are documents that are very similar that need to be processed. These situations will heavily impact your indexing strategy (which will be discussed in Chapter 5). Or suppose that emails are to be processed. Or how to deal with blather. In many ways, the source data drives many of the design decisions that will be used to process the data.

One of the important functions of the Textual ETL is that of screening out non useful unstructured data. There are no rules whatsoever for the usage and recording of unstructured data. Consequently, it is only normal that some unstructured data be irrelevant to the business of the corporation. This irrelevancy is especially true for emails, but can be true elsewhere. For example, the email: "What is the tee time on Saturday? 9:00 AM?" has little or nothing to do with the mainline business of the corporation (unless of course you are a PGA professional.)

Allowing irrelevant unstructured data to reside in the unstructured data warehouse causes the unstructured data warehouse to become bloated. In a bloated data warehouse, useful data hides behind non useful data. As unstructured data is loaded into the data warehouse, filtering out the irrelevant data becomes an important function of the Textual ETL environment.

In addition to selecting only useful data, the extraction process requires several considerations from the analyst and developer:

- **Frequency of Execution**. An important issue that needs to be decided is how often data will move from the unstructured environment through textual ETL into the unstructured data warehouse. In some cases, the unstructured data only needs to pass through Textual ETL once. In others, unstructured text must pass through Textual ETL on a periodic basis. And in yet other cases, there is so much unstructured text that even though Textual ETL processing only needs to be done once, it must be done in iterations because there simply is so much unstructured text that a single pass through Textual ETL is not viable. The analyst/designer needs to know the frequency and schedule of the usage of Textual ETL (usually determined by the IT organization) in order to prepare the system, making sure that system resources will be available when needed. Stated differently, if the analyst/designer does not take into consideration the resources that will be needed for textual ETL processing and the scheduling of those resources, he/she may be in for a shock when the textual ETL cannot be run when needed because of a lack of available resources.

- **Date Standardization**. Date standardization needs to be specified if you want to read and index dates. People create dates in text in many different forms. Trying to get a Business Intelligence engine to understand the many different forms of date is not normally something you want to do. Instead, you can specify date standardization and textual ETL will convert the dates it encounters to a common format. If you specify date standardization, you also have to specify which date format is to be used should the system encounter a date whose interpretation is ambiguous. For example, suppose the system encountered "09/12/10". Does this date mean December 9th, 2010? Or does it mean September 12, 2010? In order to properly interpret its meaning, you must specify which way of interpreting the date is to be used when it's unclear to the system.

- **Preprocessing Raw Text**. Occasionally it is necessary to pre-scan text so that the system will be able to process it. For example, suppose a text contains the words "table tennis". If the system reads those words, it is going to process them as two separate words, rather than as a phrase. And maybe that is what you want the system to do. But suppose you want the system to recognize "table tennis" as one word, specifying a sport that the Chinese are very good at. Preprocessing can be used to merge "table tennis" into one 'word', "table_tennis" in the text. All future processing will treat the phrase as one word, not two separate words. Of course, preprocessing needs to be done only when the system can only handle words, not phrases.

Another possibility is to require the textual ETL software to do spell checking. Limited types of spell checking can be done by the textual ETL technology. Numeric text transformation is another activity that you may need textual ETL to perform. Suppose in the raw text you have "one hundred". What does a query tool do when confronted with "one hundred"? A query tool usually doesn't do much except treat the phrase as just that – a phrase. The textual ETL tool can be used to convert numeric text references into true numeric references. For example, textual ETL can be used to convert "one hundred" into "100". Or textual ETL can convert "three thousand fifty two" into "3052". In doing so, the Business Intelligence tool has a value that it understands and can interpret.

Transforming Text (The 'T' of ETL)

Textual integration is the process of reading text, picking out the salient aspects of the text, and discarding the rest. There are many aspects of textual integration that apply to transforming unstructured text, which will be discussed in this section. See Figure 4.4.

Figure 4.4 The 'T' of ETL (Transform)

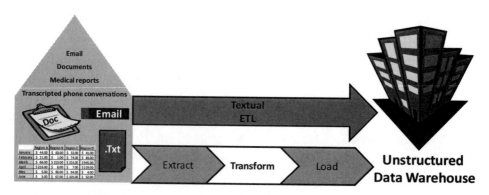

There are two styles of textual transformation: document fracturing and named value processing. Document fracturing refers to the accessing of the document as a whole and addressing stop words, stemming, alternate spelling and external categorization. Named value processing examines the document for certain words and phrases, and upon finding one of those words or phrases, the processing indexes the words or phrases that have been found. These are the two most basic ways of describing the activities of Textual ETL.

WORDS AND PHRASES

One of the basic characteristics of any worthy textual integrator is that of being able to handle both words and phrases.

Figure 4.5 A textual integrator must be able to handle both words and phrases

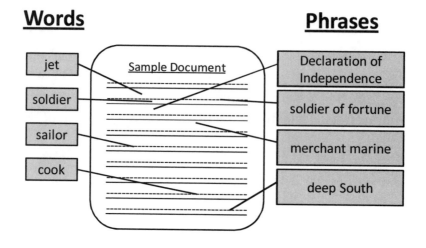

If a textual integrator can only handle words, then a big part of analytical processing is being missed. Figure 4.5 shows that in order to be considered industrial strength, a textual integrator must be able to handle both words and phrases.

As an example of being able to handle both words and phrases, consider the phrase "Glory Hallelujah." If a search is done on separate words "glory" and "Hallelujah", then the search will turn up such results as "Glory Road", "the Hallelujah Chorus", and "the mining shaft known as the glory hole." These references are very different from the expression "Glory Hallelujah." In order to enhance the results of analysis, the integration software must be able to look at not just words, but also phrases, as well.

STOP WORDS

The simplest of the parameters to set is the stop word parameter. Stop words are those words that are extraneous to the meaning of the discussion. Typical stop words in English are "a", "and", "the", "was", "is", "then", "that", and so forth. The stop word parameter states that stop words are to be removed from the document.

The stop word list can be examined, and it will be seen that standard stop words "a", "and", "the", "was", "is", and so forth, are in the list. These words can be removed from the list, if desired, and other words can be added to the list. And of course, if you are operating in other languages, you can choose a stop word list that is for the language that you want to process in.

If the parameter for stop word processing is set on, stop word processing is the first processing that occurs, so that all other processes will operate without stop words being in the document.

CASE

One of the most basic activities of Textual ETL is that of allowing a search or analysis for data to be either case sensitive or case insensitive. There are some instances where case sensitivity is desired and others where case sensitivity is not desired. The Textual ETL must be able to accommodate both circumstances. Figure 4.6 shows the need for both instances as part of Textual ETL processing.

Figure 4.6 Case sensitivity

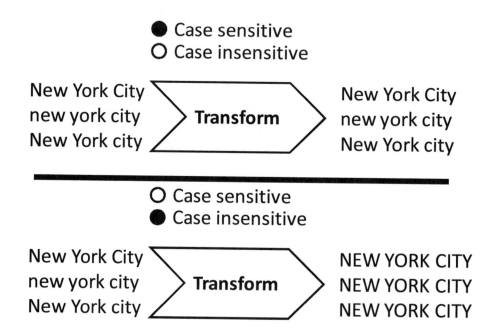

PUNCTUATION

Another similar aspect of Textual ETL processing is that of removal of punctuation. If a query is made literally, punctuation may become a problem. Therefore, when it comes to Textual ETL processing, punctuation must be removed from consideration. As an example, suppose a query is made looking for "Harper's Ferry". If the query looks for "Harper's" with an apostrophe, a match may or may not be made. (If Harper's is spelled without an apostrophe, the search won't find it.) A surer way to proceed is to look for "Harpers Ferry" where a hit is made with punctuation removed. In the interest of finding different and a wider set of hits, punctuation is best removed.

Figure 4.7 shows the practice of removal of punctuation by Textual ETL.

Figure 4.7 Removal of punctuation

FONT

If punctuation can become an impediment to successful analysis of unstructured data, so may its font. If a query looks at a specific font literally, then the query may miss many legitimate instances where a hit should have been made but wasn't because of a mismatch of fonts.

For example, a query is done for all instances of "Wimbledon", where Wimbledon is in Arial font. The analysis would miss all instances of "Wimbledon" where the text is not in Arial font – even an instance "Wimbledon" in Arial Black font would not be retrieved. Beware of font-sensitive search engines.

STEM

The next simple parameter is the stemming parameter. The stemming parameter allows words to be read and then reduced to their root word. The word that is being processed remains in the index, while stemming adds a new word. For example, suppose that in the base of unstructured data, the words "moved", "mover", "moving", and "moves" were found. If a proper analysis were to be done, it makes sense to reduce these words to their common base "move".

Care must be taken in specifying stemming to make sure that if stemming is specified for a language other than English, the stemming algorithm has been installed for that language.

The reduction to a common base is typically done in one of two ways: through a stemming algorithm such as the Porter algorithm, or though a list of words and stems.

Figure 4.8 shows that words that have a Latin base are recognized and reduced.

Figure 4.8 Reduction of words to their root

SYNONYM REPLACEMENT
==

Another important transformation is recognizing that some words are synonyms or close synonyms. Figure 4.9 shows that the word "writing" has been recognized as a synonym of "signing", "signatures" is a synonym of "autographs", and that the replacement has been made.

Figure 4.9 Synonym replacement

Synonym replacement is not used often because it entails the destruction of the original raw text. In the example shown, if someone wanted to look for "autographs", they would not be able to find the term since it has been replaced.

Much more common is synonym concatenation. Instead of replacing the raw text term that has been recognized as a synonym, the synonym is concatenated. Figure 4.10 shows such a concatenation.

Figure 4.10 Synonym concatenation

ALTERNATE SPELLING

An important parameter that can be specified is that of alternate spelling. Alternate spelling allows the system to find one word and write another index entry that is spelled differently. For example, suppose that the system encounters the word "Karen" and we want the system to alert the analyst that "Karen" can have more than one spelling. The analyst specifies in the alternate spelling table the names:

"Kairen"

"Karyn"

"Caryn"

"Caren"

as alternate spellings of "Karen".

Now, when the system is in execution, and the system encounters the name "Karen", the system inserts index entries for "Kairen", "Karyn", "Caryn", and "Caren" as well. Now the analyst that searches the indexes will find all of the spellings of "Karen".

CONCEPTUAL ABSTRACTIONS

Similar to synonym replacement or concatenation is elevation to a new level of abstraction. Abstraction occurs when a word is tagged as part of a higher level of abstraction. Figure 4.11 shows that manifestations of the abstract concept of 'perform' can be recognized and that the abstract concept can be added to the text when an appropriate word or phrase is found.

Figure 4.11 Abstract concept added to the text

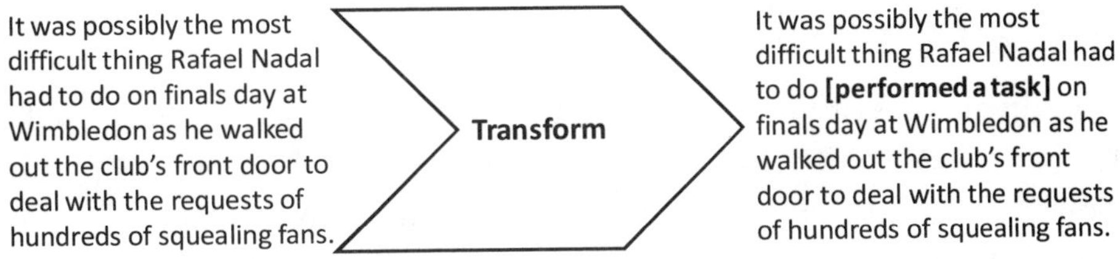

It was possibly the most difficult thing Rafael Nadal had to do on finals day at Wimbledon as he walked out the club's front door to deal with the requests of hundreds of squealing fans.

Transform

It was possibly the most difficult thing Rafael Nadal had to do **[performed a task]** on finals day at Wimbledon as he walked out the club's front door to deal with the requests of hundreds of squealing fans.

HOMOGRAPHIC RESOLUTION

Another parametric control that can be specified is that of homographic resolution. Homographic resolution occurs when a mnemonic or abbreviation is used in the text and is "translated" into its actual meaning. In homographic resolution, a homograph and its resolved value are created. When the system encounters the homograph, the system reproduces the resolved value in the index, based on the context in which the raw text was found.

Figure 4.12 shows a form of homographic resolution in which the raw text contains the term "C4". Based on the context of C4, the term is extended to its actual text meaning.

Figure 4.12 Homographic resolution

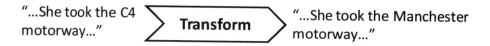

"...She took the C4 motorway..." → **Transform** → "...She took the Manchester motorway..."

NEGATIVITY EXCLUSION

Another parametric possibility is that of negativity exclusion. In negativity exclusion, an index entry is NOT created if, in the raw text that is being processed, the word is preceded by a negative word, usually "no" or "not". In negativity exclusion, no index entry is created if a negative word precedes it in a sentence.

It is one thing to index a word, but occasionally you do not want to index it if it is used in the context of a negative expression. Negativity exclusion is useful in the case where only positive references are to be indexed. In some cases the negativity is obvious, while in others, it is difficult to detect. For example, this phrase would not be indexed due to negative exclusion: "It was certainly not the dispatch of his opponent 6-2, 6-4, 6-2."

INLINE ADDITIONS

It is always possible to allow inline additions of text to be added to the raw text before the text is integrated. In Figure 4.13, inline addition of text has been made. Inline additions are often done manually. Only rarely are they done in an automated manner.

Figure 4.13 Inline addition of text

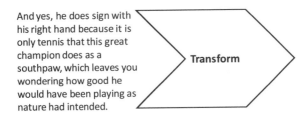

In addition to inline additions of text being made before integration occurs, inline deletion of raw text may also take place. Figure 4.14 shows that inline deletion of text has been done.

Figure 4.14 Inline deletion of text

With the ability to do inline editing before the raw text is integrated goes the ability to consolidate text. In Figure 4.15, an email string has been read. The text from the separate email strings is concatenated into a single document. In such a manner, the textual ETL software can process the logically related text together.

Figure 4.15 Consolidation of text

RECOGNIZING EXTENSIONS OF A CONCEPT

One of the most useful aspects of textual ETL is the ability to recognize extensions of a concept. For example, suppose an organization was interested in finding all the places for which Sarbanes Oxley was relevant. Note that this is quite different from finding all references to Sarbanes Oxley. The raw text is examined and everywhere there is a reference to which Sarbanes Oxley is relevant, the term "Sarbanes Oxley" is concatenated. In doing so, a query for all of the text that is relevant to Sarbanes Oxley can be performed. An example of a section of text where "Sarbanes Oxley" would be concatenated is: "We have decided to delay shipment for now. We hope this will not affect revenue recognition. We can account for this by using a transaction structured as a contingency sale."

PATTERNS

Another valuable parameter that can be set is the patterns parameter. The patterns parameter specifies that as the system looks through words, it should look for the pattern, recognize it as a variable, and write out the index reference and the contents of the index. For example, suppose the system has 999-999-9999 specified as a pattern for a telephone number. When the system encounters the number 303-682-6882 in raw text, it would write out "Index – telephone number, value – 303-682-6882".

There are two basic forms of pattern recognition: standard and custom. A standard pattern is one that is commonly found in text, such as an industry standard. A custom pattern is one that is described on a custom basis by the analyst/designer. For example, a standard email address is in the form of xxx@yyy.com. Or a custom pattern might be in the form of a part number xx-99xx-999.

PROXIMITY ANALYSIS

With proximity analysis, the system looks for two words that are within a specified number of bytes to each other. The parameters specifying Word A and Word B are set, followed by setting the parameter for the byte differential. The system then looks for all occurrences of the two words within the specified byte differential. The described activity yields a proximity variable.

For example, if Word A is "party" and Word B is "dinner" and the byte differential is "100", the phrase "...The party is a dinner party" would be returned.

CLUSTERING

Clustering variables is essentially the same thing as proximity variable processing except that proximity variable processing operates on two words and clustering variables operates on three or more words. On occasion it is useful to find where clusters of words are, rather than just to find a word or two. Finding clusters of words in close proximity is called cluster analysis.

In cluster analysis the contents of one or more documents are gathered, and an analysis of the frequency of the words in the document and the proximity of those words to each other is performed. A cluster analysis is done strictly on the basis of the contents of the specific document or documents being analyzed.

Loading Text (The 'L' of ETL)

After transforming the text, you are finally ready to start setting the parameters for loading text. See Figure 4.16.

Figure 4.16 The 'L' of ETL (Load)

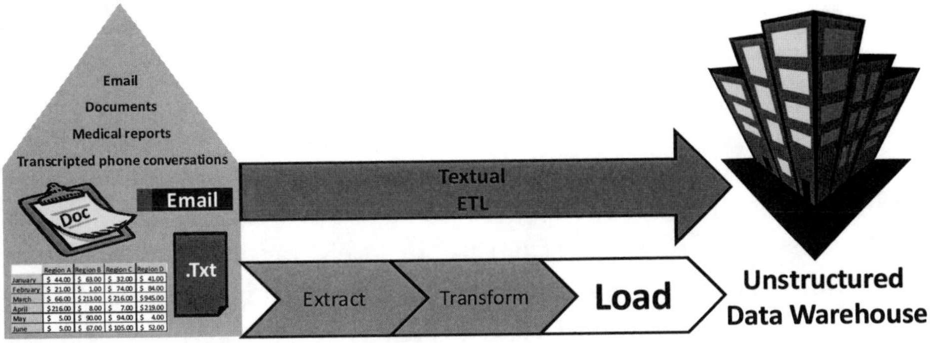

USING THE MOVE/REMOVE UTILITY

If you are building the unstructured data warehouse from scratch, after transforming the text you are going to have to define the parameters that will instruct Textual ETL how to read and interpret the raw textual data that you will be feeding it. The first parameter(s) that need to be set are the text editing parameters. (If these parameters do not need to be set, then don't set them.) Sample text editing parameters include whether or not to do stemming, alternate spelling, stop word processing, homographic resolution, and so forth. Note that you only have to define the parameters that you will actually be using. There may be many parameters that don't need to be defined because the parameters are not relevant to the processing that you will be doing.

One of the considerations of loading text that was created by textual ETL is the ability to restore the analysis that was done. If, for example, at a later point in time you lose the data that was created, you may need to do the analysis once again. In order to repeat the analysis, it is wise to store the parameters that were used to create the analysis. You don't want to have to recreate the parametric definition that governs the processing of Textual ETL again. Therefore, a preliminary step to loading the data created by textual ETL is to "save" the parameters used for the creation of the data. This is akin to the first step of "backup and recovery".

When you are ready to start defining parameters for a new analysis, you need to first check and see if any parameters have already been defined that will suit your purposes. If the unstructured input that you will be using has already been used (perhaps someone has already built a similar unstructured data warehouse), then many (or even all) of the parameters needed may have already been defined. By reusing parameters, you can save a lot of your own time.

In order to determine if parameters have already been defined, look for the parametric move/remove utility. The parametric move/remove utility is used to store sets of parameters that describe one document when the document is finished processing. When it comes time to process the same or similar type of document again, the parameters that are stored by the move/remove utility can be recalled, rather than having to be recreated. With this utility, you will be able to determine whether or not parameters have already been defined. If, in fact, parameters have already been defined (in whole or in part), then they can simply be moved from the move/remove storage area into the Textual ETL parameter area.

REVIEWING THE OUTPUT TABLES

The tables into which the unstructured data will be stored should be reviewed before building the unstructured data warehouse. The sorts of questions that need to be reviewed include:

- Can the volume of data be accommodated?
- Will the type of data being entered into the unstructured data warehouse fit the types of indexes that are being planned?
- How will the different tables of data relate to each other?
- How easy (or difficult) will it be to query the tables that are being created?

There are many different ways that unstructured data can be structured. The analyst/designer needs to make sure that the tables that are planned will meet the needs of most queries.

KNOWING THE FINAL DESTINATION

Before the unstructured data warehouse is built, the analyst/designer needs to know in which database management system (DBMS) the unstructured data warehouse will be built.

There are many considerations to the building of the unstructured data warehouse in a standard database management system. Some of the considerations are:

- **How large will the unstructured data warehouse be?** Some DBMS accommodate one volume of data, while other DBMS accommodate another level of volume of data. For example, SMP-based DBMS (that is, symmetric multi processing) can handle moderate volumes of data and MPP-based DBMS (that is, massively parallel processing) can handle very large amounts of data.
- **How many analytical tools are available to operate on the unstructured data warehouse?** Some DBMS have many analytical tools that support operating against the DBMS, while others have only a limited number of tools for analytical processing. Some typical analytical tools include SAS, Business Objects, Crystal Reports, and MicroStrategy.

- **What cost is there to building and using the unstructured data warehouse in the DBMS?** Some DBMS are more expensive than others, with very high ongoing costs associated with their usage, while other DBMS have a lower cost associated with their ongoing usage.

Knowing what the final DBMS destination of the tables that will be built by textual ETL is an important consideration.

MANAGING VOLUMES OF DATA

The analyst designer needs to have a fairly good understanding of the volume of data that will be loaded into the unstructured data warehouse. It is easy for an unstructured data warehouse to grow in size far faster and far larger than anyone ever imagined. The analyst/designer needs to consider such things as:

- How easy will it be to load the unstructured data warehouse?
- What alternatives are there to reducing data (or partitioning data) should the unstructured data warehouse grow larger than expected?
- Is it possible to pull only limited amounts of indexed data into the unstructured data warehouse rather than large amounts of data?
- Is stop word processing to be used?
- Has simple indexing been considered?
- Has data been analyzed according to its probability of access?

Ultimately, the unstructured data warehouse can have unlimited growth as long as someone is willing to pay for the resources that are needed. Often times, the end user community wants huge amounts of data until they are told that they have to pay for it and what it costs. All of a sudden, they discover that they can get by with far less data than what they had originally envisioned.

Not only does the initial size of the unstructured data warehouse need to be considered, but its growth rate needs to be considered as well.

Estimating the size of data that will go into the unstructured environment is more of an art than a science. A lot of time can be wasted in trying to create a very exact projection of the size of the data that will be needed in the unstructured data warehouse when only a very rough estimate is needed at the beginning. As a very general rule, the data found in the data warehouse will be approximately 60% of the size of the raw data. This is, however, dependent on many factors such as the amount of blather and whether stop words are removed.

PERFORMING CHECKPOINT PROCESSING

A final consideration is that of needing to do checkpoint processing. When a lot of documents are being processed, or when an especially large document is being processed, it may be desirable to do checkpoint processing. When processing is checkpointed, the system can always return to the last record that was created and resume processing there. If processing stops for whatever reason, all the work that has already been done will be retained. There is no need to go back and reprocess work that has already been done.

Textual ETL Examples

There are many kinds of unstructured data, but (arguably) the most pervasive forms of unstructured data are email and spreadsheets. An interesting aspect of email and spreadsheets is that each of these forms of unstructured data has their own idiosyncrasies. Given that emails and spreadsheets are ubiquitous and given that each has its own idiosyncrasies, a closer examination of extracting, transforming and loading these forms of unstructured data is in order.

EMAIL

The first issue of emails is that of privacy. Before ANY processing of emails is done, the question should be asked, is it legal for an organization to be processing the text found in emails. The laws of countries vary around the world with regard to an organization looking at and processing emails. The last thing any analyst/designer wants to happen is to wake up one day and find out that they have been breaking the law. Therefore, the first step in processing emails is to ascertain that no laws will be broken.

The second consideration for processing emails is that of making sure that email attachments can be processed along with the email. In many cases, the email attachment has more useful information than the email, itself. Therefore, a very early consideration of email processing is to ensure that the attachments of the email can be processed along with the email, itself.

A third and very important consideration of processing emails is that of the content of the email. Most emails contain only a scant amount of information. The end user must have the proper expectations set as to the depth and value of the analysis that can be done with the contents of the email. It is a mistake to assume that wondrous sorts of analysis can be done from emails when the information found on the emails is not profound. When an email is created for personal purposes, it has no business use and takes up space and processing cycles. The analyst is well advised to remove all blather from the email queue as one of the first steps in processing emails. Otherwise, valuable time and resources are taken up in processing emails that are not useful or meaningful.

The question then arises is how to remove blather from the email stream? There are many techniques for doing this. The one that is discussed here is but one of many approaches.

One approach to the removal of blather from the email stream is to pass the emails through a screen. The screen determines whether the email contains business relevant information or not. The dynamics of the screen work like this. Each email is passed through the screen. The words in the email are examined and, if they are useful to the business, then the email is considered to be business relevant. But if the words in the email are not relevant to the business, then the email is deemed to be blather.

The words that are used to determine business relevance are those that come from one or more business related taxonomies.

Figure 4.17 shows the process of screening emails for business relevance.

Figure 4.17 Screening emails

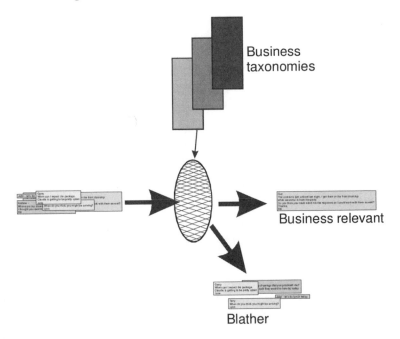

The emails that are deemed to be blather are sent to one queue. The emails that are determined to be business relevant are passed on to textual ETL for further processing.

Once the business relevant emails are passed to textual ETL, they are treated like any other form of unstructured text.

It is noteworthy that the emails of the corporation are reduced to words that are useful for analytical processing which are then added to the unstructured data warehouse. All sorts of analytical processing can take place against the text found in the emails, but the actual email is not stored in its entirety in the unstructured data warehouse, it still resides at its source. If, after processing text in the unstructured data warehouse, it is necessary to look at the original emails, then returning to the source of the email and looking at it directly is supported.

As a final note, the amount of space that a collection of emails can use up can be considerable. Care must be taken not to let the volume of emails overwhelm the unstructured data warehouse.

SPREADSHEETS

The second form of data that is pervasive is that of spreadsheets. In truth, there are many challenges with using spreadsheets as a source of data. Nevertheless, with care, spreadsheets can be used as input to textual ETL.

The first (and overwhelmingly important) consideration of using spreadsheets as input to textual ETL is to constantly remember that spreadsheets are divided into units called "cells". There are many reasons why cells are important, but the most important reason is that the cell that a unit of data resides in provides context. Each numeric cell in a spreadsheet has an underlying formula in a spreadsheet, and it is this formula that gives the cell its meaning.

For example, suppose you have a cell that has the value 723. The value 723 means nothing without understanding the formula that was used to calculate the number. But the formula for the calculation of the cell is not apparent when you look at the cell and its value. If you understand that the number 723 was calculated by adding up the shipments for a day, then the value 723 takes on meaning. But without understanding the underlying formula for a cell, the contents of the cell means nothing.

Unfortunately, the underlying value for a cell is not available for processing when you strip the values from a spreadsheet. Because of this, the value of a cell that is numeric is frequently not useful.

A second important consideration of spreadsheets is that their format and structure are not normally uniform across an organization. Each person has his/her own spreadsheet and the form and structure of the spreadsheet is unique to the individual.

Because of the lack of context for any given cell and because of the uniqueness of the structure and format of the spreadsheet to an individual, processing spreadsheets as input to the textual ETL process must be done carefully and judiciously.

Having stated that there are definitely some limitations and challenges to the use of spreadsheets as input to the textual ETL process, spreadsheets can, nevertheless, be used as input. This section will discuss the different ways of acquiring data from spreadsheets, including stripping cells, rows, and columns, as shown in Figure 4.18.

Figure 4.18 Stripping spreadsheet cells, rows, and columns

	Region A	Region B	Region C	Region D
January	$ 44.00	$ 63.00	$ 32.00	$ 41.00
February	$ 21.00	$ 1.00	$ 74.00	$ 84.00
March	$ 66.00	$213.00	$216.00	$945.00
April	$216.00	$ 8.00	$ 7.00	$219.00
May	$ 5.00	$ 90.00	$ 94.00	$ 4.00
June	$ 5.00	$ 67.00	$105.00	$ 52.00

Cells can be stripped

Rows can be stripped

Columns can be stripped

Stripping off all the Cells

A simple way to get data from a spreadsheet into textual ETL is simply to strip off all cells. From a mechanical standpoint, this approach is quite straightforward.

But there is a serious problem with merely going into a spreadsheet and stripping off all the cells, then entering those cells into a Textual ETL input job stream. That problem is that once the cells are stripped off, they lose their meaning. Textual ETL has no way of interpreting a cell that has a value of 723. So, while it is possible to strip all cells from a spreadsheet, it is usually meaningless to do so.

Stripping off all Alphabetic Cells

A somewhat refined approach is to ignore all cells that have non numeric values. But if a cell contains a non numeric value, then it is included in the Textual input job stream. This means that only alphabetic data is entered into Textual ETL. Sometimes a spreadsheet will have a lot of alphabetic data that is appropriate for entry. But even then, there is no understanding of what one cell represents versus another cell. As long as the analyst/designer doesn't care what is represented, then such a transfer of data suffices.

Stripping off Cells by Column

A more meaningful way to enter cells of data from a spreadsheet into textual ETL is to move cells by columns. There are two ways to specify that a column should be entered. One way is to specify the spreadsheet column designation column A, column B, column C, and so forth, or to specify the text at the heading of the column. Specifying either way has its disadvantages. When the spreadsheet column specification is used, the specification is precise. But if more than one spreadsheet is entered as input, then all spreadsheets must use the same column specification for the same data. Given that spreadsheet formats and structures usually vary from one user to the next, making the assumption that all users specify the same column for the same thing is a large and often untrue assumption.

But specifying a column name has its own drawbacks. When the specification of a column name is made, the column name must be unique. If, for example, the column name is "TOTAL", then the input to Textual ETL will pick up ALL column names named "TOTAL". That may not be what the analyst/designer had in mind.

In addition, if more than one spreadsheet is entered and the analyst /designer wishes to pluck the same data from all spreadsheets, then all spreadsheets must use the same column name. If one spreadsheet has "TOTAL" and another spreadsheet has "MONTHLY TOTAL" then Textual ETL is not going to recognize these totals as the same type of data.

Nevertheless, specifying an individual column of cells is better than merely selecting all cells from a spreadsheet.

Stripping off Cells by Row Number

Another alternative for selecting text from a spreadsheet for inclusion into the Textual ETL input job stream is to select cells of data by row number.

One way to specify row number is by the spreadsheet row number. The spreadsheet row number might be 1,2,3, and so on. When the spreadsheet row number is used, it is certainly precise. In addition, it may be desirable to select a range of row numbers from 3 to 17, for instance. But selecting row number has its disadvantages, too. The appropriate row number may change from one spreadsheet to the next. And even for the same spreadsheet, the row number may change every time a new row is entered. So specifying the spreadsheet row number is hardly an ideal alternative.

Another way to specify row number is to specify that a row is selected by the content of a given cell. For example, suppose that all appropriate cells for selection in column 1 start with the text "DELEGATE". The analyst/designer can specify that the text "DELEGATE" be used to determine which rows should be entered. By choosing a term that is common to all rows that should be selected, the analyst/designer can easily and quickly select all the appropriate rows for inclusion into the Textual ETL input job stream.

Stripping off a Single Cell

Yet another alternative is that of selecting a given cell for inclusion into the textual input job stream. In this case, the row and column must both be specified. The same approaches to specifying the row and column can be used as described above. The difference is that both a row and a column must be specified. In doing so, the system can focus in on a single cell for inclusion into the Textual ETL input job stream.

As the Cell Arrives in Textual ETL

When the cell, any cell, arrives at the point of entering textual ETL, the cell needs to contain several pieces of information. It needs:

- The cell contents
- The row the cell came from
- The column the cell came from
- Identification of the spreadsheet the cell came from.

Frequently, the non cellular content of data takes up more space than the cellular content. Yet the non cellular information is absolutely crucial for the end user analyst to determine the meaning of the data that has been captured.

It has been shown that both emails and spreadsheet data can be entered as input into the Textual ETL job stream. However the analyst/designer must be aware of the many considerations surrounding the effective use of the information found in emails and spreadsheets.

Key Points

- The entire objective of integrating text is to support analytical processing against this text. Integration processing must be able to handle both words and phrases.

- The source data drives many of the design decisions that will be used to process the data. Common sources of unstructured data include corporate servers and desktops, the Internet, paper, and transcriptions.

- One of the guiding principles when reading unstructured data is that once read the unstructured data should not be read again, unless modifications have been made to the unstructured data.

- Consider many factors when transforming text, including phrase recognition, case, stem, and alternate spellings.

- Checkpoint processing is very useful when loading data.

The unstructured data warehouse is built in a methodological fashion like all other aspects of the information infrastructure. The methodology for building the unstructured data warehouse is a combination of the classical development and spiral approaches.

SDLC

The classical development methodology is called the SDLC or "system development lifecycle." The classical development methodology is shown in Figure 5.1.

Figure 5.1 System development lifecycle

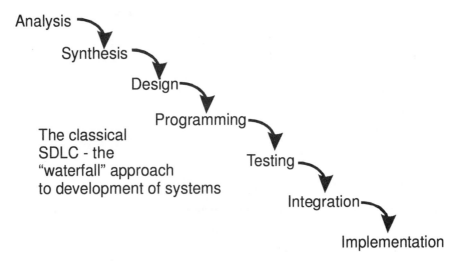

In Figure 5.1 it is seen that there is a linear progression from the early stages of design and development to the final stages. Development proceeds from one stage of development to the next in a "waterfall" manner. The next stage of development does not start until the preceding step is complete.

Spiral Approach

In contrast to the SDLC is the spiral development approach. In the spiral approach, the steps of development occur very quickly and many different iterations of development occur. The scope of any given iteration is small and the iteration is completed quickly. Figure 5.2 shows the classical spiral development approach.

Figure 5.2 Spiral development approach

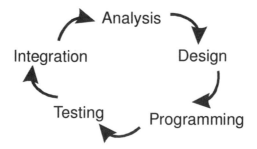

The development approach for the unstructured data warehouse is a combination of both of the approaches to development.

Hybrid Approach

Combining both the SDLC and spiral approaches leads to these eleven steps that will be described in detail in this section:

1. Understand the business problem and business context
2. Survey the data sources to determine which data is useful
3. Select and customize taxonomies
4. Select the initial set of data
5. Determine future iterations and source document requirements
6. Choose the textual ETL tool
7. Load parameters for transformations
8. Execute ETL scripts with initial set of data
9. Examine results and make adjustments, if needed
10. Execute ETL scripts on remaining iterations
11. Continuous business analysis and make adjustments, if needed

1. UNDERSTAND THE BUSINESS PROBLEM AND BUSINESS CONTEXT

The first step in the development of the unstructured data warehouse is that of defining its general business requirements and context. The business context of the unstructured data warehouse has many far reaching implications. When the general context of the business behind the unstructured data warehouse is known, many design decisions become obvious.

In truth, the first time that an unstructured data warehouse is built, there may be more questions than answers as to its worth. The estimate of the business worth may be no more specific than something like "retail customer support". Or the projection of the business worth may be very specific, such as support for the Hart-Kinsley lawsuit. In any case, it is very helpful to have an understanding of the business use of the unstructured data warehouse, as the business value often shapes its form and structure.

As an example of understanding and identifying the business context of an unstructured data warehouse, an organization could state that the context of an unstructured data warehouse may be:

- All information relevant to litigation relating to a product line or a product failure
- Medical research done by a healthcare organization
- All information relevant to safety inside the organization
- Loans portfolio analysis.

2. SURVEY THE DATA SOURCES TO DETERMINE WHICH DATA IS USEFUL

The second step in building the unstructured data warehouse is that of identifying all sources and potential sources of unstructured data. Here, the analyst/designer can become creative. News articles, research, hospital visits, police records, insurance claims, and so forth, are all potential sources for an unstructured data warehouse, depending on its business context. Some of the observations that need to be considered here include:

- The volume of data to be input
- Whether the input is available at the outset or will be arriving over time
- The structure of the input data – repetitive or non repetitive, how robust is it, is it in well-structured sentences or in comments?
- The language of the documents – English, Spanish, French, and so on.

3. SELECT AND CUSTOMIZE TAXONOMIES

After the sources of input are surveyed, the next step in building the unstructured data warehouse is the selection and preparation of taxonomies. As discussed earlier, taxonomies are only needed when terminology resolution is an issue or when categories of text must be assigned. There will be occasions when taxonomies are not needed. But if they are needed (which is the usual case), then they need to be identified now.

When taxonomies are needed, how much of the taxonomy that is needed must be identified, as well. It is normal for a taxonomy to contain far more terms than are necessary. When more terms are selected than necessary, there is a performance penalty to be paid. That penalty can be mitigated by weeding out unnecessary terms from the taxonomies that have been selected. The analyst configuring the taxonomies uses business common sense to weed out unnecessary words and phrases in the taxonomy.

The taxonomies that are selected should be relevant to the business context of the unstructured data warehouse. If the business context of the data warehouse were medical records, it would be unusual to select a taxonomy for golf, religion, or weather, for example.

4. SELECT THE INITIAL SET OF DATA

Step 4 in the building of an unstructured data warehouse is to start by choosing a very small subset of data to begin the development process. If the data resides on paper, then an OCR process needs to be initiated.

The purpose of selecting a small subset of data to start with is to make sure that if there are insurmountable or unexpected problems with the data, they are recognized as soon as possible. The subset that is selected should be small but representative of the range of data that will be brought into the unstructured data warehouse.

Certainly all potential problems will not be discovered in this step, but if there are large, unforeseen problems waiting, they should be identified as soon as possible.

5. DETERMINE FUTURE ITERATIONS AND SOURCE DOCUMENT REQUIREMENTS

After the small subset of data has been selected and examined closely, and there are reassurances that no insurmountable problems await, the next step is to outline the steps of iteration that will take place. Under no circumstances is it advisable, or even desirable, to try to build the unstructured data warehouse all at once in a "big bang" approach. Instead, the unstructured data warehouse should be built in a series of small, fast iterations.

The iterations of development should be planned from the beginning. The sequence of the steps, the time each step is allotted, and the disposition of the output of ETL processing should be identified here.

It is possible to develop different components of the unstructured data warehouse in parallel. One development team will be working on one part of the unstructured data warehouse while another team works on another part. If that is the case, then there must be a concerted effort to insure that coordination of the efforts be done carefully and properly. Stop word lists, taxonomies, indexing and so forth, must all be compatible if parallel development efforts are the plan.

6. CHOOSE THE TEXTUAL ETL TOOL

After the iterative development plan has been developed, it is time to select a tool for Textual ETL. Each organization needs to determine its own criteria and priorities for a tool. Some of the criteria for the selection of the tool may include the ability to:

- Handle large volumes of data
- Create the data warehouse in a multiplicity of technologies
- Read in and manage many different input sources
- Do external categorization
- Do sub document processing
- Do basic editing, such as alternate spelling and data standardization
- Do named value processing
- Do proximity analysis and clustering
- Operate in multiple languages
- Handle iterations of data
- Do pattern recognition
- Do document fracturing
- Do semi structured processing
- Do process comments as well as well formed sentences
- Handle stop words
- Read in spreadsheets
- Read in and filter email
- Support preprocessing
- Support post processing editing
- Support document metadata capture
- Support homograph processing
- Support document classification
- Support many different types of indexing.

Once the textual ETL tool has been selected, then a "burn in" time is needed (as with any software). The textual ETL tool must be installed and the connections to the network must be in place. Space must be allocated and a few test cases need to be run. Training on the tool is necessary.

7. LOAD PARAMETERS FOR TRANSFORMATIONS

After the ETL tool has been selected and burned in, the next task is to create the parameters that will tell the system how to integrate the data. As was discussed previously, there are many parameters that can be set. Some of them are:

- Select delimiters for named value variables
- Identify homographs
- Modify external category entries
- Do preprocessing
- Select extension types.

If previously defined parameters are applicable, they can be downloaded from the storage area using the Move/Remove utility. Because of the Move/Remove utility, it is necessary to specify the bulk of the controlling parameters only once.

8. EXECUTE ETL SCRIPTS WITH INITIAL SET OF DATA

After the execution parameters are loaded, it is time to execute the Textual ETL software. If the parameters are loaded properly, executing the Textual ETL software and producing the first set of results is easy.

9. EXAMINE RESULTS AND MAKE ADJUSTMENTS IF NEEDED

The next step is to look at the results, comparing the textual input with the output. The output from the textual ETL processing is in the form of a relational data base. Simple query tools can be used to examine the processing results. It is normal for there to be omissions and misunderstandings between how the parameters are set and how the results will look. Adjustments are made and the results are recreated. (Note: because it is normal for there to be adjustments, it is apparent that operating on large amounts of data in the first several passes is a mistake.)

10. EXECUTE ETL SCRIPTS ON REMAINING ITERATIONS

Once the parameters are set properly, the many iterations of transformation are performed. Each iteration will produce its own output. The different sets of output are gathered as the iterations are run.

When the last of the iterations are run, the different sets of results are combined into a grand final result and put into the final output DBMS (such as Oracle, Teradata, DB2, or SQL Server).

11. CONTINUOUS BUSINESS ANALYSIS AND MAKE ADJUSTMENTS IF NEEDED

Now the analysis can begin. The end user can start to use any analytical tool desired and can perform any analysis desired. It is to be expected that upon doing analysis, the end user will suggest changes and additions, and parts of the development cycle will be revisited.

If a stream of raw data is created on a regular basis, then the initial development work and the setting of parameters will only have to be done once. Once a new job stream is created, it can be operated on using previously prepared parameters.

Putting the Steps Together

Taken as a whole, there are some parts of the unstructured data warehouse development methodology that are done once in the style of the classical SDLC, and there are other parts that are done repetitively in the style of the spiral development methodology. Figure 5.3 shows approximately how the steps should be executed.

Figure 5.3 Sequence of the steps

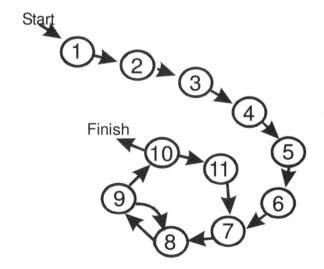

As with all methodologies, there are exceptions to the rule. The methodology described here, like all methodologies, is designed to represent a general pattern of how processing should occur. While there is nothing cast in concrete with this methodology, an analyst/designer should carefully consider his/her reasons before taking a drastically different approach.

Key Points

- The methodology for the building of the unstructured data warehouse is a combination of the classical development and spiral approaches.

- Under no circumstances is it advisable, or desirable, to try to build the unstructured data warehouse all at once in a "big bang" approach.

- It is possible to develop different components of the unstructured data warehouse in parallel.

SECTION II
Unstructured Data Warehouse Advanced Topics

This section covers more advanced topics on building the unstructured data warehouse. Specifically, by the end of this section, you will master these objectives:

- Design the Document Inventory system and link unstructured text to structured data
- Leverage indexes for efficient text analysis and taxonomies for useful external categorization
- Manage large volumes of data using advanced techniques, such as the use of backward pointers
- Evaluate technology choices suitable for unstructured data processing, such as data warehouse appliances.

Chapter 6 describes how to inventory documents for maximum analysis value, as well as link the unstructured text to structured data for even greater value. The Document Inventory is discussed, which is similar to a library card catalog used for organizing corporate documents. This chapter explores ways of linking unstructured text to structured data. The emphasis is on taking unstructured data and reducing it into a form of data that is structured. Related concepts to linking, such as probabilistic linkages and dynamic linkages, are discussed.

Chapter 7 goes through each of the different types of indexes necessary to make text analysis efficient. Indexes range from simple indexes, which are fast to create and are good if the analyst really knows what needs to be analyzed before the indexing process begins, to complex combined indexes, which can be made up of any and all of the other kinds of indexes.

Chapter 8 explains taxonomies and how they can be used within the unstructured data warehouse. Both simple and complicated taxonomies are discussed. Techniques to help the reader leverage taxonomies, including using preferred taxonomies, external categorization, and cluster analysis are described. Real world problems are raised, including the possibilities of encountering hierarchies, multiple types, and recursion. The chapter ends with a discussion comparing a taxonomy with a data model.

Chapter 9 explains ways of coping with large amounts of unstructured data. Techniques such as keeping the unstructured data at its source and using backward pointers are discussed. The chapter explains why iterative development is so important. Ways of reducing the amount of data are presented, including screening and removing extraneous data, as well as parallelizing the workload.

Chapter 10 focuses on challenges and some technology choices that are suitable for unstructured data processing. The traditional data warehouse processing technology is reviewed. In addition, the data warehouse appliance is discussed.

Most companies have a wealth of unstructured textual information. There are documents of many kinds found in many places: reports, articles, spreadsheets, contracts, and so on. Intuitively, the organization knows that it ought to be doing something with these documents. Trying to find a document six months after it was written is no small task. Trying to gather documents for a cost justification or for litigation support is not trivial. Most corporations have never even attempted to manage their corporate documents. Yet some of the most valuable information the corporation has is found in documents. Documents are like small minnows in the water - they keep multiplying and they are slippery to catch.

Not all corporate documents need to be managed. Many informal documents and presentations do not warrant being managed. But many documents do need management. Many corporate documents represent official pronouncements and statements of obligations and expectations by the corporation.

Document Inventory

A good first place to start for an organization that wants to proactively manage its documents is to create a corporate document inventory. In creating an inventory, the organization looks at and catalogs its existing documents. In some organizations, there are literally hundreds of thousands of documents. Building a "card catalog" of the documents that belong to the organization is an excellent way to start managing the corporate collection of documents. See Figure 6.1.

Figure 6.1 Library card catalog

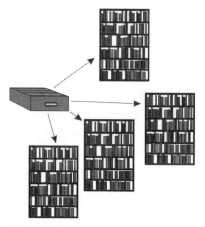

The card catalog saves ENORMOUS
amounts of time

Libraries have long used a card catalog to great effect. Libraries know that looking through an entire library with all of its books is a colossal waste of time. Realistically, if it were not for the card catalog, libraries would not be in existence. When a person is looking for a book in the library, the most efficient way to look for the book is to use the card catalog. With the card catalog, the reader can quickly scan through all the possibilities. Upon finding the one or two books that look the most promising, the reader is then directed to the location of the book by the card catalog. And it is no different with the documents that belong to the corporation.

So what should an inventory of corporate documents – a corporate card catalog - contain? The corporate card catalog should include information such as:

- A title or brief description of the document
- A measurement of the size of the document
- The date the document was created
- The date the document was last changed
- The date the document was last accessed
- The system path of the document
- A classification of the document type.

Figure 6.2 shows the kinds of information that belong in a document card catalog.

Figure 6.2 Kinds of information in a card catalog

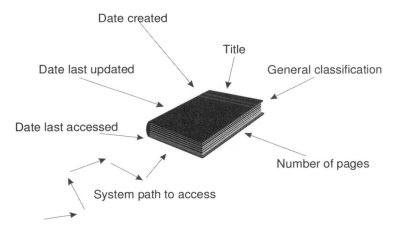

Date created

Title

Date last updated

General classification

Date last accessed

Number of pages

System path to access

All of these components of the card catalog are useful. Indeed some, but not all, of the elements of the card catalog are found in the metadata of the document. Perhaps the most useful of the card catalog elements is the document classification.

Document Classification

Documents can be classified in many ways. Consider an oil company. The business of the oil company can be roughly divided into the sectors of "upstream", "mid stream", and "downstream". Upstream refers to the process of exploration. Mid stream refers to the process of refining and pipeline. Downstream refers to the process of distribution. Each document that belongs to the oil company can be read and classified into the general category of information that the document contains. The document can be an "upstream" document, a "mid stream" document, or a "downstream" document.

Or consider manufacturing. In manufacturing, there is the process of handling raw goods, assembly, managing work in process, finishing a product, and shipping or storing the product. Documents for manufacturers can be classified as to which aspect of manufacturing the document best applies to. Classifying the content of the document is a jump start for the analyst looking through the many documents that belong to the corporation.

Creating an inventory of corporate documents is an activity that represents the first start to managing the unstructured environment. Stated differently, without a corporate card catalog, the world of unstructured data is a massive blob of ambiguity.

After an inventory is made, the next step is to read the documents and create a corporate index of them. The index doesn't just reflect the document classification, it goes into the details of every word in every document. There are many and varied aspects to the creation of an index. Some of the aspects are:

- Looking at and managing documents in different languages
- Classifying the content of documents so that there is a "higher" level of abstraction for each word and each concept in each document
- Taking information found in documents and organizing that information so that textual analytics can be supported
- Organizing the information found in documents and creating the index so that it can be queried along with structured information.

Indeed, there are many different aspects to creating the corporate card catalog.

One of the challenges is that of dealing with different document types. Some documents are short (emails). Some documents are long (patents). Some documents are full of technical jargon (medical or legal documents). Some documents are full of slang (chat logs). The corporate card catalog needs to be able to accommodate *all* of the different kinds of documents.

Linking Unstructured to Structured Data

For years, the world of business intelligence has centered on doing analytical processing of structured data. Structured data is typically transaction based. There are many very useful and interesting things that can result from analysis of structured data. But imagine an entirely new form of analysis where it is possible to include both unstructured data and structured data in the analysis. Whole new questions and whole new perspectives of analysis are possible where the two worlds can be linked together.

The first step in linking the worlds together is taking unstructured data and reducing it into a form of data that is structured. This book has described how that is done with textual ETL. Raw text goes into Textual ETL and a classical relational database may be created with the output.

But placing unstructured data in a standard relational database is not the only requirement for analytical processing that encompasses both structured and unstructured data. Another requirement is the ability to logically link the structured and the unstructured worlds.

Linkage of different units of data from multiple databases has long been done. Figure 6.3 shows a common kind of linkage that can be found in many systems.

Figure 6.3 Database referential integrity

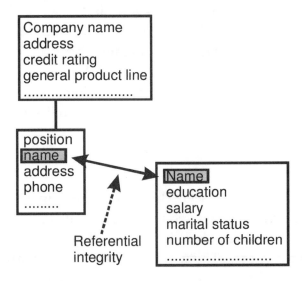

Standard databases have long supported key/foreign key relationships. In relational technology, the technology used to support such a relationship is called referential integrity. In a standard key/foreign key relationship, the relationship is binary. Either the relationship exists or it does not.

If Bill Inmon is a customer of a bank, then there will be a relationship between the account for Bill Inmon and the personal record for Bill Inmon. But if Bill Inmon is not a customer of the bank, there will be no record from an account to a personal record. Stated differently, Bill Inmon is either a customer or he is not, so the probability of a relationship is either 1 or 0.

Having a binary relationship is normal for key/foreign key relationships, and key/foreign key relationships are normal for structured data.

A PROBABILISTIC LINKAGE

It is possible to form a linkage between the unstructured world and the structured world in many different ways. However the linkage is formed, it has a special property. The linkage between the structured world and the unstructured world is not a binary link at all, it is a probabilistic link, which is quite different from a binary relationship.

A probabilistic link is one that has a probability of being true. If the probability is 25%, then there is a low probability that the linkage has a valid business relationship behind the rule. If, on the other hand, the linkage probability is 90%, then there is a good chance that there is a valid business rule behind the linkage. A low probability of linkage is said to be a weak link. A high probability of linkage is said to be a strong link.

A Weak Link

In Figure 6.4, it can be seen that somewhere in the unstructured environment, text that says "you must pay your bill." is found. In the structured environment, there is a record that says "Bill Inmon, Yale University, Golfer, etc." The word "bill" appears in both places. It can be inferred that there is a business relationship between the environments based on the appearance of the same word in both places. While the inference can be made, the odds are very good that there really is no business relationship. The linkage shown in Figure 6.4 is a very weak link. The probability of there being a real business relationship here are almost nil.

Figure 6.4 Weak link

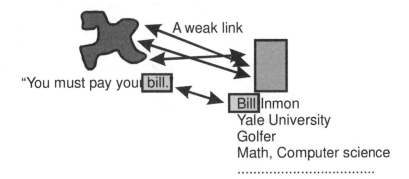

A Strong Link

The link in Figure 6.5 shows that the same email address exists in both the structured and the unstructured environment. Unlike the word "bill" appearing in both places, when an email address appears in both places, the chances are pretty good that there is a business relationship between the structured and the unstructured environment. The linkage shown in Figure 6.5 is a strong link.

Figure 6.5 Strong link

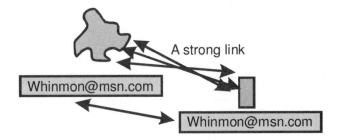

Now consider the linkage shown in Figure 6.6.

Figure 6.6 Very strong link

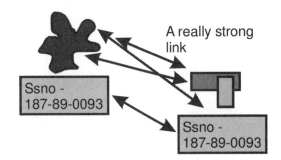

The link shown in Figure 6.6 is an even more powerful link. The link here is a social security number. The same social security number is found in the structured and the unstructured environment. The chances of there being a business relationship in the structured environment and the unstructured environment are very, very good.

It is interesting to note that a strong linkage between the structured environment and the unstructured environment does not necessarily imply anything about the business relationship that is behind the linkage. The only implication is that there is a relationship, but that relationship could be almost anything.

DYNAMIC LINKAGES

The implementation of linkages can be accomplished in several ways. One way the linkages can be implemented is dynamically. In a dynamic linkage, the linkage is created "on the fly" by a transaction or query. At the moment the query goes into execution, the query looks first for one part of the linkage and then for the other part. If both parts of the linkage are found, then the linkage is considered to be complete.

By making the calls to the structured and unstructured environments as a part of the query, the data that is being accessed is always accurate up to the second. The problem with a dynamic linkage is that making calls to the different environments may entail the use of a lot of resources. The calls may cost a lot of resources if they generate full table scans. So, on the one hand, a dynamic linkage always operates on up to the second accurate data, but does so at the potential expense of a lot of resources. Figure 6.7 shows a dynamic implementation of linkage.

Figure 6.7 Dynamic linkage

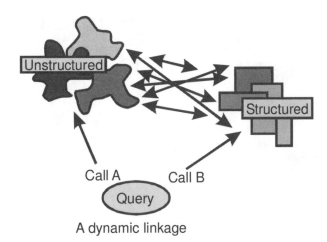

A dynamic linkage

STATIC LINKAGES

Another implementation of the linkages between the structured and the unstructured environments is one that is called a static link. In a static link, a program examines both environments and searches for the existence of a relationship. If a relationship is found, an index entry is made.

When it comes time to access the linkage, it is easy and efficient to do so. A simple query of the index will determine whether a link exists or not. The downside of a static link is that if the unstructured environment or the structured is in a state of flux, then the index that is created may not be accurate for very long. Stated differently, if many updates or insertions are being made to either the structured or the unstructured environment, then the index that is created will become inaccurate very quickly.

DYNAMIC VERSUS STATIC

Both types of linkages have their advantages and disadvantages. Either the index needs to be constantly repaired or the analyst making the query needs to live with the fact that the index may be out of date. Neither a static nor a dynamic link is the proper choice in and of itself. The context of usage determines the correctness of the choice. Table 6.1 shows the tradeoffs of using static versus dynamic linkages.

Table 6.1 Comparing dynamic and static linkages

	Disadvantage	Advantage
Dynamic linkage	Slow to process	Up to the second accuracy
Static linkage	Fast to process	Requires building and maintaining an index

Key Points

- Building a "card catalog" of the documents that belong to the organization is an excellent start to managing the corporate collection of documents.

- Whole new questions and whole new perspectives of analysis are possible where unstructured data and structured data can be linked together.

- Relationships between the structured and the unstructured world are probabilistic relationships, which can be strong or weak links.

- In a dynamic linkage, the linkage is created "on the fly" by a transaction or query. A static linkage is created by a program that examines both environments and searches for the existence of a relationship.

The ability to read and capture unstructured data and to organize it into a meaningful, useful database is of unquestionable value. However, that value becomes really apparent in the face of actual analysis and queries. Stated differently, the value of creating an unstructured data warehouse becomes really apparent when there is a need to query unstructured data.

The general architecture of how analytical processing is done is illustrated by Figure 7.1.

Figure 7.1 General analytical processing architecture

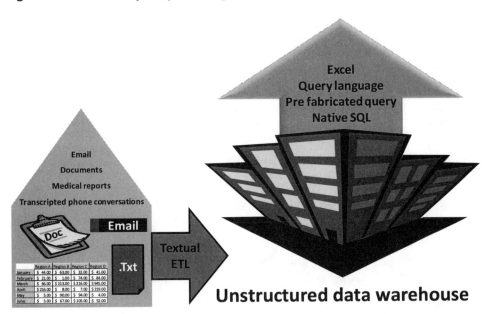

In Figure 7.1 it is seen that unstructured data is fed into textual ETL. Textual ETL processes the text and creates an unstructured data warehouse. Once the unstructured data warehouse is created, the analytical processing can be done against the unstructured data in several ways: Excel spreadsheets can be created, a query language can be used, queries can be prefabricated, or even native SQL can be created. In fact, there are many other ways that queries can be created and that analysis can be done.

The style of analysis depends on a lot of factors. One factor is what kind of data is in the unstructured data warehouse and how much data there is. Another is the sophistication of the end user. Unsophisticated users often depend on prefabricated queries, while sophisticated users may write their own SQL or statistical queries.

There are many places where the output of analysis can be stored. Some of these places are:

- In the workstation where the analysis is taking place
- On disk storage in a database or simply stored as an individual data set
- Sent on email, where the results are passed to another person by means of email
- In a report, where the output is used as a basis for a report.

There are many forms of analysis. In one form the analyst is looking for just a single result who wrote a check for $59.16 last Thursday? In other cases, data is gathered for further analysis – how many orders were there in February for more than $500.00? Depending on the question being answered, the analyst can look at data in many different ways.

Textual ETL is the process by which raw text is converted into a structured database format. Textual data is read into Textual ETL and indexes are created. An index is an arrangement of selected units of data placed in an order that is quickly and easily accessible to the user. That is a simple statement of fact. But there are some very sophisticated and some not so sophisticated indexes that can created. The indexes that are needed so that text can be analyzed properly are actually quite varied.

Depending on the input source data and on the final use of the data, the analyst shaping the unstructured data warehouse is free to choose which index structure or structures best fit the needs of the data warehouse and the uses of data within the data warehouse.

There are many different types of indexes that can be created as a result of processing unstructured data. There is no one right or wrong index. Instead, the proper index type is one that fits the unstructured input and the ultimate use of the unstructured data warehouse. In this chapter we will be discussing these index types:

- Simple
- Fractured
- Named value
- External category
- Patterned
- Homographic
- Alternate spelling
- Stemmed words
- Clustered
- Combined

Simple Index

The simplest kind of index that is needed is the "simple index". In a simple index, the data that is placed in the index is specified before the index is created. In other words, the user identifies what is of interest to him/her before the index is created. The analyst determines that Word A, Word B, Word C, and so forth, are of interest before the indexing process commences. The system then passes through the text and determines the location of all of the occurrences of Word A, Word B, Word C, and so forth.

Simple indexes are fast to create and are good if the analyst really knows what needs to be analyzed before the indexing process begins. The problem with simple indexes is that it is costly for the analyst to change his/her mind at a later point in time. If the analyst wakes up one morning and discovers that some other word(s) need to be found and indexed, then they can either add the new word to the index or recreate the entire index. Either way, a complete new scan of data is necessary to add the new word.

In a simple index, the analyst/designer tells the system what words or phrases need to be indexed. The system then creates the indexes on the words and phrases that have been chosen. As long as the end user analyst does not wish to see anything other than the predetermined words and phrases, simple indexes work just fine.

Figure 7.2 shows the dynamics of a query made on a simple index.

Figure 7.2 Simple index

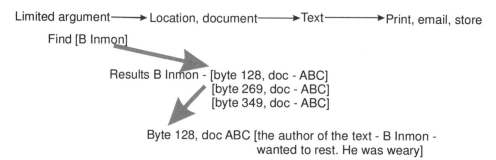

In Figure 7.2, the end user analyst wishes to see information about "B Inmon". Assuming that an index has been created for names, a search of the index indicates three entries for "B Inmon" have been found. Using the byte address and the document designation, the actual text is located. For the first occurrence of "B Inmon" that was found, the text surrounding "B Inmon" is located.

Fractured Index

Simple indexes are fine as long as you don't want to look for anything that hasn't been indexed. Unfortunately, most analysis and most searches extend well beyond the bounds of any predetermined indexes. When a more expansive analysis needs to be done, simple indexes will not suffice. Instead, the next step up is a document fractured index. In a document fractured index, everything is indexed (except stop words). Document fractured indexes require more resources to build and more storage than a simple index, but once having been built, a document fractured index can support very expansive types of analysis.

The document fractured index is one where a document is taken in its entirety, stop words are removed, and all remaining words are indexed. On occasion, alternate spelling processing, external categorization, and stemming are done before the document fractured index is created. With a document fractured index (also known as a "fractured" index) all non stop words are indexed. This takes considerably more time and space than building a simple index, but the analyst using the index at a later point in time has much greater flexibility than if the simple index were created. The analyst can choose to analyze anything that he/she wants when a fractured index is created.

Figure 7.3 shows a document fractured index and the analysis that can be done against it.

Figure 7.3 Fractured index

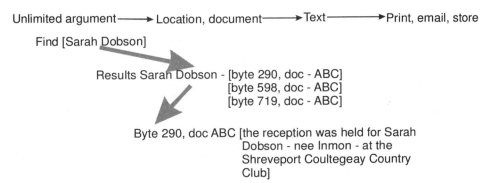

Figure 7.3 shows that a name is being searched: "Sarah Dobson". The difference between the query and analysis done in Figure 7.2, where a simple index is being used, and Figure 7.3, where a document fractured index is being used, is that with a document fractured index, *any* query can be supported, whereas with a simple index *only* queries that operate against predetermined fields of data can be indexed.

The dynamics of the query done in Figure 7.3 are essentially the same as the dynamics of the query done in Figure 7.2.

Another type of common query often found associated with document fractured indexes is a compound query. In a compound query, two arguments are passed to the search engine, along with a byte specification. This triggers a search for the two arguments where they appear in the text within the byte limitation that has been specified. This type of query is often called a proximity query because it looks for two arguments that are in close proximity to each other. Figure 7.4 shows a compound query.

Figure 7.4 Compound query

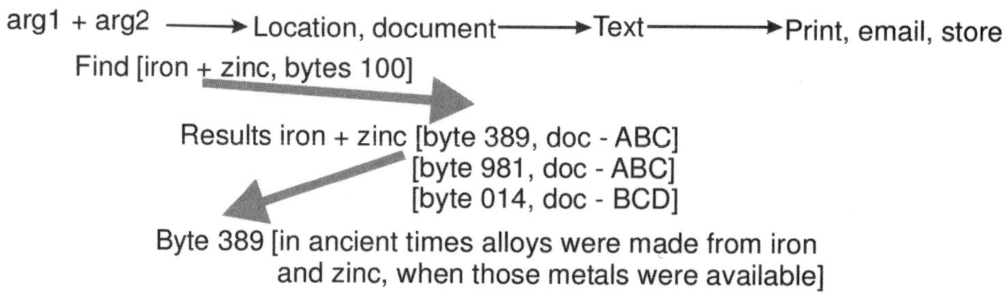

arg1 + arg2 ⟶ Location, document ⟶ Text ⟶ Print, email, store
Find [iron + zinc, bytes 100]

Results iron + zinc [byte 389, doc - ABC]
[byte 981, doc - ABC]
[byte 014, doc - BCD]

Byte 389 [in ancient times alloys were made from iron
and zinc, when those metals were available]

In Figure 7.4 the arguments "iron" and "zinc" are passed to the search engine along with the byte specification of 100 bytes. The search looks for both "iron" and "zinc" where these words are within 100 bytes of each other.

In Figure 7.4 there are three occurrences found. Looking at the text for the first occurrence that was found, indeed a reference to iron and zinc in ancient times is located where the words are x bytes apart, which is within the 100 bytes specified.

Named Value Index

Another kind of index that can be created is the named value index. The named value index is created by identifying beginning and ending delimiters. The value found between the beginning and ending delimiters is then chosen for the index value.

Named value indexes are most frequently used where there is much repetitive information. A named value index has the added benefit in that not only is the index created, but the name of the index is known as well. For example, suppose that an analyst has a collection of resumes. The analyst may use named value index processing to identify the names off of the resumes. In doing so, one type of index can be separated from another type of index. For example, on resumes there may be indexes on name, address, telephone, education, and so forth. Suppose that the analyst/designer wishes to identify all the education that a person has had by looking at the resume. The analyst/designer might specify "EDUCATION" as the beginning delimiter and "EOL" (the character for end of line) as the ending delimiter. In such a manner, an index for education would be created and the value contained in the resume would be created as an index entry.

But suppose that some resumes had the word "TRAINING" rather than "EDUCATION". In this case, the analyst/designer would specify that the index for Education would have a beginning delimiter of "TRAINING". In such a manner any index may have multiple sets of delimiters that apply.

With named value indexes, a different kind of search can be done. Named value indexes allow you to search on types of data. With simple indexing and document fractured indexes, a search is done on a specific value. With named value indexes, a search can be done on types of data, not specific values of data. Figure 7.5 shows a named value index.

Figure 7.5 Named value index

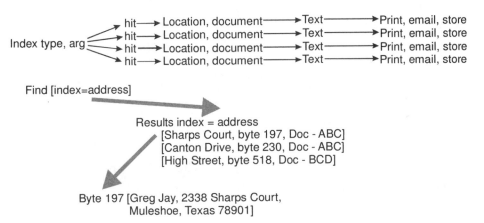

In this query, the analyst wishes to find all addresses. Note that with a simple index or a document fractured index, the search was for a particular word. Here, the search is for a word type – address. The query on word type "address" returns three results. Following the byte and document designation leads to the text that contains the address.

Looking for text by means of word type is one way to use a named value index. However there are other searches that can be created as well. Figure 7.6 illustrates one of those ways.

Figure 7.6 Other ways to leverage the named value index

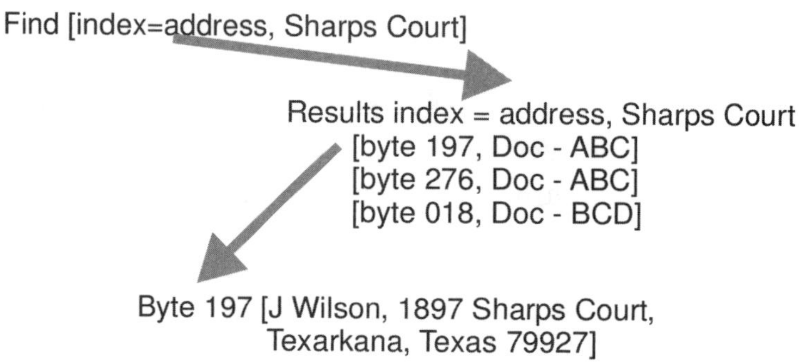

Find [index=address, Sharps Court]

Results index = address, Sharps Court
[byte 197, Doc - ABC]
[byte 276, Doc - ABC]
[byte 018, Doc - BCD]

Byte 197 [J Wilson, 1897 Sharps Court,
Texarkana, Texas 79927]

In Figure 7.6, the search against the named value index specifies that the word type "address" be used and that the specific address for "Sharps Court" be sought. Figure 7.6 shows that there are three places where "Sharps Court" is found. Note that the word "Sharps Court" could be found in other places in the document, as well. Only those places where "Sharps Court" is recognized as an address are returned by the query. With named value indexing, the system can recognize where an address exists and where there is no address.

Taxonomy (or External Categorization) Index

Another type of index is the external category index, or a "taxonomy" index. (Taxonomies will be discussed in Chapter 6). An external category index is created based on the selection of words in a category. For example, suppose there is a simple category of words for CAR:

CAR

> Porsche
> Volkswagen
> Cadillac
> Honda
> Ford

When the external category processing encounters the name of a car in the category, the system writes out a taxonomy record. For example, suppose the system found the word "Honda" in the text. The system recognizes Honda as a car because it is in the taxonomy for CAR. The system then writes out two records: one for Honda (which the system would have written out in any case) and another index record for Honda as a car. In such a manner, an external category index record is produced.

In accessing an external category, the query is made against an argument and all the external categorizations related to the external category are accessed. Figure 7.7 shows an external category query.

Figure 7.7 External category index

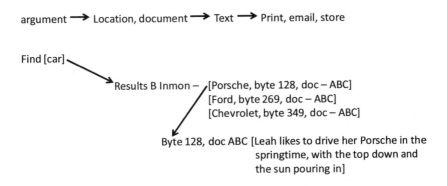

In Figure 7.7 a query is made on "car". The query on "car" results in three car types being found: Porsche, Ford, and Chevrolet. Following through to the text, it is seen that text references Leah and how she drives her Porsche.

External categories can be used for many purposes. One purpose is to define a "meta-language". In this case, synonyms or closely related words are grouped together by an external category. The query shown in Figure 7.8 shows such a grouping.

Figure 7.8 Using an external category index to define a "meta-language"

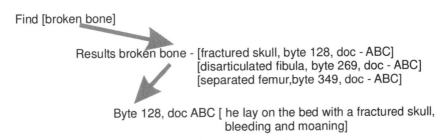

In the query shown in Figure 7.8, the term "broken bone" is sought. The different forms of broken bones found in the document that are

located by the query are fractured skull, disarticulated fibula, and separated femur. When an external category is used in this manner, the external category forms a sort of "meta-language".

Or another use of external categorization occurs when the analyst/designer wishes to group together different words or phrases that belong to a class of activities. For example, suppose the analyst/designer wishes to look at all the activities of Sarbanes-Oxley. The analyst designer could create a category for Sarbanes-Oxley, then underneath that category have text such as "delayed delivery", "revenue recognition", "pre ship product", and so forth. In such a manner, the analyst can refer to the category "Sarbanes-Oxley" and find all the references to the activities to which Sarbanes-Oxley applies.

External categories are normally created from taxonomies. The appropriate taxonomies are created by reading text, creating a fractured document, taking selected words from the fractured document, formatting the words, and then entering them into Textual ETL. Following this, the analyst/designer selects the parameter for External Categorization.

Care must be taken when choosing External Categorization in that if the External Categories contain lots of entries, the time to process them through textual ETL can be excessive.

Patterned Index

Another important index type is the patterned index. A patterned index is created when a common pattern is found and recognized. On occasion, the type of word is recognized merely by looking at its format. Some simple examples are:

- (American) telephone number – 999-999-9999
- Email address – xxxx@yyyy.com
- Social security number – 999-99-9999

When the pattern is recognized, the index value and the type of pattern are created in the index table. Figure 7.9 shows a patterned index.

Figure 7.9 Patterned index

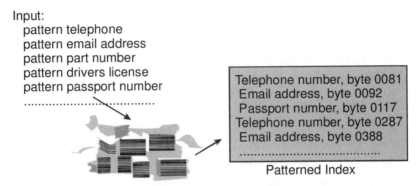

Input:
    pattern telephone
    pattern email address
    pattern part number
    pattern drivers license
    pattern passport number

Telephone number, byte 0081
Email address, byte 0092
Passport number, byte 0117
Telephone number, byte 0287
Email address, byte 0388

Patterned Index

Homographic Index

Another important type of index is the homographic index. As its name suggests, a homographic index is one where the homographs in the text are indexed. For example, as mentioned earlier, suppose the raw text has the value "ha" in the context of medical records. If the person writing the text were a cardiologist, the term "ha" is interpreted to mean "heart attack". If the person writing "ha" were a general practitioner, the term "ha" would be interpreted to mean "head ache". If the person writing the term "ha" were an endocrinologist, then the term "ha" would be interpreted to mean "hepatitis A".

When a homograph is recognized, its interpretation is indexed, thereby greatly aiding the analyst who will use the indexed data. Figure 7.10 shows a homograph search.

Figure 7.10 Homographic index

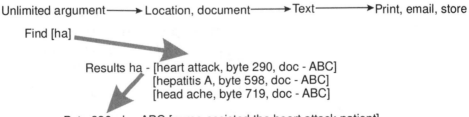

Unlimited argument ⟶ Location, document ⟶ Text ⟶ Print, email, store

Find [ha]

Results ha - [heart attack, byte 290, doc - ABC]
          [hepatitis A, byte 598, doc - ABC]
          [head ache, byte 719, doc - ABC]

Byte 290, doc ABC [nurse assisted the heart attack patient]

In the search that is shown, the term "ha" is supplied as an argument. The results of the argument search include the terms "heart attack", "hepatitis A", and "head ache".

Alternate Spelling Index

Another type of index is the alternate spelling index. The alternate spelling index is one in which an argument is supplied for a search, but the search results include all alternate spellings of the argument. The raw text is read and upon encountering any of the alternate spellings, the index is created for all spellings.

Figure 7.11 shows an example of a search for alternate spellings.

Figure 7.11 Alternate spelling index

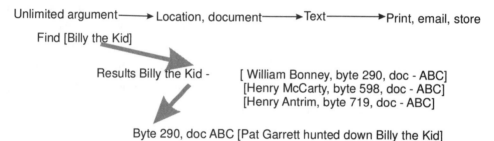

Unlimited argument ⟶ Location, document ⟶ Text ⟶ Print, email, store

Find [Billy the Kid]

Results Billy the Kid -   [William Bonney, byte 290, doc - ABC]
[Henry McCarty, byte 598, doc - ABC]
[Henry Antrim, byte 719, doc - ABC]

Byte 290, doc ABC [Pat Garrett hunted down Billy the Kid]

In the example shown in Figure 7.11, the argument being sought is "Billy the Kid". The alternate spellings of "William Bonney", "Henry McCarty", and "Henry Antrim" are all returned as a result of the alternate spelling search.

Stemmed Words Index

Yet another form of indexing is one based on a stemmed word. An argument for a stemmed word must be provided. The argument is reduced down to its Latin or Greek stem, and all other like stems are provided as a result of the search. The index is created based on the stem of the word. Note that the stem of the word may or may not be a word itself. For example, the stem of the words "moving", "moved", and "mover" is "mov". And of course "mov" is not a word, but it is a stem of a class of words. Figure 7.12 shows a stemmed query.

Figure 7.12 Stemmed words index

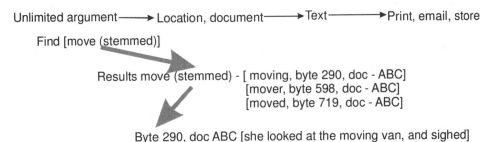

In the search shown in Figure 7.12, it is seen that the argument "move" is passed to the search along with the request for a stemmed search. The results of the search turn up the words "moving", "mover", and "moved" as words all emanating from the same word stem, "mov".

Clustered Index

Yet another type of index is one based on clusters of information. In an index based on clusters of information, three or more words are supplied as an argument and the byte limit is supplied as well. The cluster is determined when the three or more words are found within the byte limitation that has been provided. Figure 7.13 shows a cluster query.

Figure 7.13 Clustered index

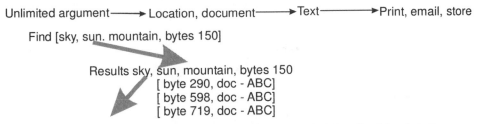

In Figure 7.13, it is seen that the words "sky", "sun", and "mountain" are provided within the byte limit of 150 bytes. The number of places where the words occur in the proximity provided by the byte limits is shown.

Combined Index

Yet another kind of index that can be created is the combined index. Combined indexes can be useful when it is desirable to have all index types combined in a single index. Having a single index is operationally more streamlined than administering multiple indexes. While all index types can be created individually, it is also possible to create an index that contains more than one index type. The combined index can be made up of any and all of the other kinds of indexes. In a combined index, there can be simple index entries, fractured index entries, named value index entries, homographic index entries, patterned index entries, and external category index entries.

It is often useful to combine different index entry types into a common combined index because the end user needs to look for a wide variety of occurrences of data. One minute the end user wants to search for a particular word, while the next minute the end user wants to search for a type of word. Then the next minute, the end user wants to search for a particular word found in a logical sub structuring of the document. Figure 7.14 shows a combined index.

Figure 7.14 Combined index

Word A, byte 0091
Homograph, byte 0118
Word A, byte 1276
....
Named Value, byte 0016
Word B, byte 0276
....
Word G, byte 0100
Data Pattern, byte 0287
....
Word K, byte 0817
....
External Cat, byte 0417
Word J, byte 0561
....
Word X, byte 0165
....

Leverage Multiple Indexing Strategies

In reality, there are many ways to build the unstructured data warehouse. By understanding the business objectives, the analyst/designer can make intelligent choices as to how to build the unstructured data warehouse. For example, if the source data is email, the designer will probably want to filter blather, do stop word processing, and create a fractured document. If the documents are contracts, the designer is likely to use named value processing and document fracturing. If the source is doctors' notes, the designer will want to use homographic resolution and external categorization, as well as alternate spelling. The nature of the source and the ultimate usage of the documents dictate the kind of textual ETL processing that will be done.

For example, suppose that a large body of text needs only to be surveyed for any reference to several words. In this case, it makes sense to build a simple index, as the simple index can be built quickly and without using many resources. By building a simple index, the analyst can quickly survey the text for the existence of the words that are of interest.

On the other hand, if a detailed correlative analysis of many factors needs to be studied, a fractured index can be built so that the analyst can look at anything that is in the text. The fractured index requires a lot more time and resources to build than a simple index. But the analysis that can be done on a fractured index is far greater than the analysis that can be done on data found in a simple index.

As another case in point, suppose the text that is run through textual ETL is to be used for general purpose business intelligence, where analytical processing will be done by a large and diverse audience of users. To support this use, it may be worthwhile to build fractured indexes, named value indexes, pattern indexes, cluster indexes, proximity indexes, and so forth.

SEMISTRUCTURED (SUB DOC) PROCESSING

Sub doc processing occurs when a document contains logical subdivisions that need to be recognized in the index. The first step in sub doc processing is that of defining the delimiter or delimiters that will specify a logical break in the document. The delimiter may be a standard character or a special character. In many cases, the delimiter is a string of characters.

The first pass through the data identifies where the delimiters are. With sub doc processing, a second pass through the data is required, during which the words that were indexed are divided into subdivisions based on the appearance of the delimiters.

Some documents have no logical sub structuring, while others do. When a document does have logical sub structuring, it is often important to be able to find and recognize that logical sub structuring.

As an example of a document that has logical sub structuring, consider a recipe book. Figure 7.15 shows a recipe book.

Figure 7.15 Sub doc pointers are created

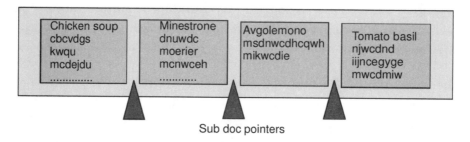

Sub doc pointers

A recipe book contains different recipes. There is, then, a natural logical sub structuring of the content of the document. The logical sub structuring of the document is demarked by showing where one recipe ends and another recipe begins.

In order to capture this information, sub doc pointers are created. The sub doc pointers mark where one recipe ends and the next recipe begins.

The sub doc pointers appear in the index and are used to break the document into its logical sub divisions. All index entries that occur from the start of the document to the first sub doc pointer are in the first logical subdivision. All index entries that are between the first sub doc pointer and the second sub doc pointer are in the second logical sub division of the document, and so forth. Figure 7.16 shows that there are sub doc pointers dividing the document up into its logical sub divisions.

Figure 7.16 Sub doc pointers divide a document

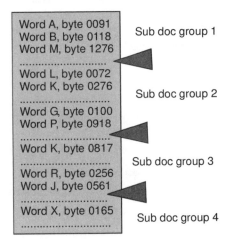

It is noteworthy that sub doc pointers can be used for ALL kinds of indexing. Sub doc pointers can be used for simple indexes, fractured indexes, named value indexes, and so forth.

When sub doc indexing is found, the basic indexing remains the same. Stated differently, a simple index that is not sub doc is the same as a simple index that is sub doc, a document fractured index that is not sub doc is the same as a document fractured index that is sub doc, and so forth. When sub doc indexing is done, the index is divided up into logical groups.

As an example of the effect of sub doc processing, consider the simple index that has been sub doc processed, shown in Figure 7.17.

Figure 7.17 Simple index that has been sub doc processed

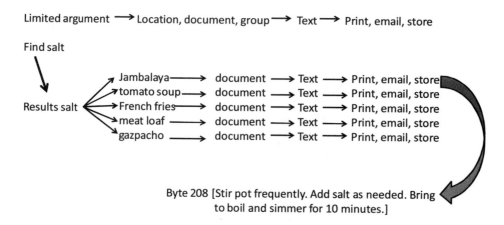

In Figure 7.17, there is a search for salt against a sub doc simple index. In the figure, the recipes that salt appears in become apparent. And once the reference is found, a trace can be made to the actual raw text. Because the index is simple, the searches can only be done against the words that were specified before the index was created.

Of course, the query can be more sophisticated. Consider the query in Figure 7.18.

Figure 7.18 More sophisticated sub doc processing

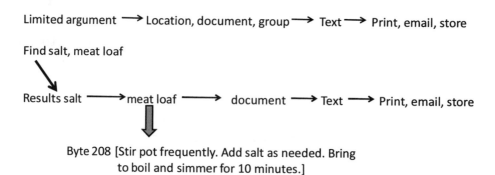

In Figure 7.18, it is seen that salt and meat loaf are specified as arguments. Salt uses the simple index and meat loaf uses the group that salt is found in. In doing so, salt in meat loaf can be used as a query argument.

Sub doc processing can be used for all sorts of indexes. One of the index types it can be used for is named value indexing. As an example of the usage of sub doc processing, consider the example shown in Figure 7.19.

Figure 7.19 Usage of sub doc processing

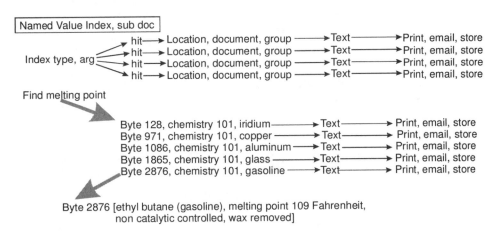

In Figure 7.19, a query is executed against a named value index where the argument is "melting point". The results show that "melting point" is found in several places and that there are groups of data in which "melting point" is found.

Of course, the query could have been refined to show that a group of data could be sought along with the word type. In Figure 7.20, the query is on the word type "melting point" and the sub doc group "glass", with the results of the query shown.

Figure 7.20 Query on word type "melting point" and sub doc group "glass"

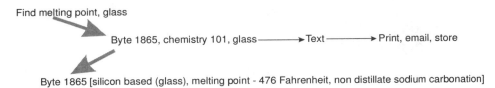

Key Points

- There are many different types of indexes that can be created as a result of processing unstructured data. There is no one right or wrong index. Instead, the proper index type is one that suits the unstructured input and the ultimate use of the unstructured data warehouse.

- Simple indexes can be created quickly and are good if the analyst really knows what needs to be analyzed before the indexing process begins.

- Document fractured indexes require more resources to build and more storage than a simple index, but once built, a document fractured index can support very expansive types of analysis.

- The named value index is an index that is created by identifying beginning and ending delimiters.

- A taxonomy index is an index created based on the selection of words in a category, such as 'car' or 'Honda'.

- A patterned index is one that is created when a common pattern is found and recognized.

- A homographic index is one where the same terms (even if they have different definitions) are indexed.

- Sub doc pointers break the document up into its logical sub divisions to retrieve sections of a document quickly.

- In a stemmed word index, the argument is reduced to its Latin or Greek stem, and all other words with the same stems are provided as a result of the search.

- The combined index can be made up of any and all of the other kinds of indexes.

CHAPTER 8
Leveraging Taxonomies

In preparation for executing textual ETL, you will need to select and prepare the taxonomies that will be used. A taxonomy, in its simplest form, is a list of categories or synonyms. Taxonomies are necessary for the creation of the "meta" layer of text used to address terminology.

If you are going to be using taxonomies, you need to select the ones that are the most germane to the unstructured data warehouse that you are building. Suppose you are building a manufacturing control unstructured data warehouse. You will probably need taxonomies on the product that is being manufactured and the manufacturing process. You will almost certainly not need taxonomies on code of ethics, Sarbanes-Oxley, recreational activities, and religion.

Furthermore, you may want to go into the taxonomies you have selected and "weed out" sections that may not be relevant to the data that is found in your unstructured data warehouse. The idea is to use the minimal number of words in the taxonomy that will suffice. The reason for this is that the usage of taxonomies requires fairly significant overhead when doing Textual ETL processing. You don't want the system spinning needless cycles by creating a taxonomy that is not relevant to your unstructured data warehouse.

It is completely normal to select more than one taxonomy for your external category processing. Most taxonomies are fairly focused and will address only one aspect of your business. In order to cover more than one aspect of your business, you are very likely going to need more than one taxonomy.

Another consideration when selecting a taxonomy is that occasionally, the format of the taxonomy needs to be altered in order to get the taxonomy into Textual ETL. Some taxonomies are represented as a hierarchical list of words, while others are represented by a series of word pairs that have one or more implicit relationships. If the taxonomy you choose needs to be altered, you usually need to use a utility to reformat it into the form and structure required by the Textual ETL technology.

Simple Taxonomy

A taxonomy, from a simplistic standpoint, is merely a list of words related to a single topic. Recall from Chapter 7 the simple taxonomy:

CAR

>   Porsche

>   Volkswagen

>   Cadillac

>   Honda

>   Ford

This simple taxonomy is a list of types of cars. One type of car is a Porsche, another type of car is a Ford, and so forth.

To say that there are almost an infinite number of taxonomies is not much of an exaggeration. Figure 8.1 shows a very small sample of the different types of taxonomies there are.

Figure 8.1 Examples of taxonomies

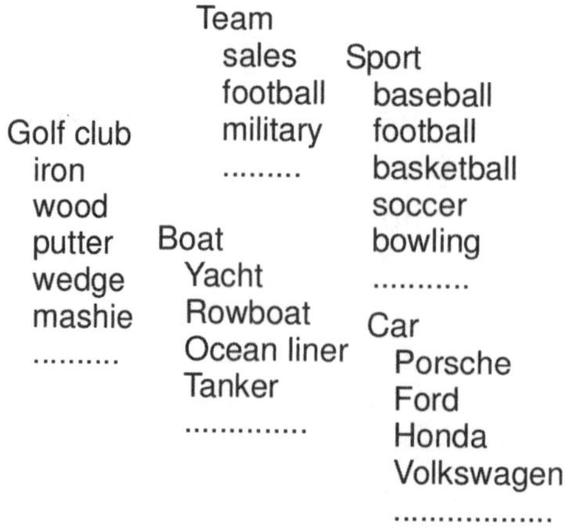

```
                          Team
                           sales    Sport
                           football baseball
         Golf club         military football
          iron             ........  basketball
          wood                       soccer
          putter  Boat              bowling
          wedge   Yacht            ..........
          mashie  Rowboat   Car
         .........  Ocean liner  Porsche
                   Tanker        Ford
                  .............   Honda
                                  Volkswagen
                                  .................
```

There are taxonomies for religion, ethics, Sarbanes-Oxley, hockey, babies, legal activities, aging, medicine, slang, and so forth. The possibilities for different categories of every object, every activity, every attitude, and every continent are endless.

When the analyst/designer begins to apply taxonomies to unstructured data, care must be taken to select the taxonomies that apply to the unstructured data that is to be analyzed. Trying to select all the taxonomies in the world is absolutely not the right thing to do.

Pairs of Words

The words in the list of the taxonomy all have the same relationship to the category of the list. Figure 8.1 shows that a Porsche, a Ford, a Honda, and a Volkswagen all have a relationship with being a car. What a taxonomy does not infer is any other relationship between the words in the list. For example, the simple taxonomy in the example does not infer a relationship between a Porsche and a Ford, or a Honda and a Volkswagen. The ONLY relationship inferred by a taxonomy is that there is a relationship between the category and the items in the list.

The relationship inferred by the category can be of almost any type. For example, one categorization relationship may be that of being a synonym. The list may contain all synonyms for the category. Or the category may refer to items that are a subset. For example, the category may be "Sarbanes-Oxley" and the words found in the taxonomy may be all the activities and conditions that Sarbanes-Oxley refers to. Or the taxonomy may be the towns and villages located in a country. The relationship between the category and the elements of the taxonomy can be just about anything.

However the taxonomy is created, it can be broken down into a series of parent/child relationships. Figure 8.2 shows that the "car" taxonomy can be broken down into a series of car-Porsche, car-Ford, car-Honda, car-Volkswagen relationships.

Figure 8.2 Car taxonomy can be broken down into parent/child relationships

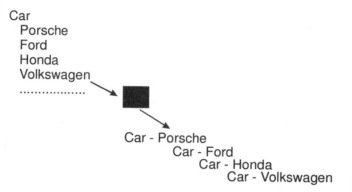

By breaking down the taxonomy into a series of parent/child relationships, the analyst/designer can simplify the taxonomy and make it fit for processing for the Textual ETL software.

And when it comes to more complex (more real world) taxonomies, those relationships can be broken down into a similar series of parent/child relationships. Figure 8.3 shows the result of breaking down a more complex taxonomy into a series of parent/child relationships.

Figure 8.3 More complex taxonomy broken down into parent/child relationships

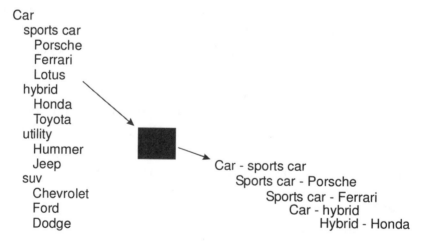

Once the taxonomy is broken down into a series of parent/child relationships, the taxonomy can be fed into the textual ETL process. Figure 8.4 shows the feeding of parent/child relationships into Textual ETL.

Figure 8.4 Feeding of parent/child relationships into textual ETL

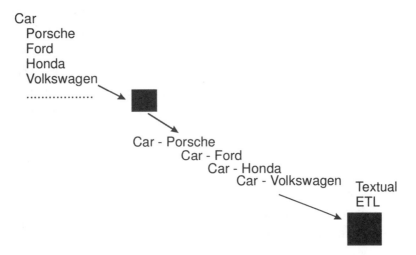

Once the simple parent/child relationships are fed into Textual ETL, it is easy to use the parent/child relationships with matching logic to convert the raw text into an index. Figure 8.5 shows that raw text is being read and that when a match is found, the categorization of the raw text is created.

Figure 8.5 Using the taxonomy to categorize raw text

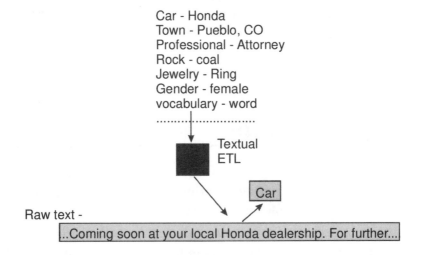

Preferred Taxonomy

Another technique used in processing with taxonomies is to specify what can be called a "preferred" taxonomy. Suppose there are multiple taxonomies specified as classifications that can be used in the understanding of unstructured text. Now one is designated as the "preferred" taxonomy – to be used before any other taxonomy is used in the resolution of text. Only after a matching effort has been made against the preferred taxonomy is a matching effort attempted against the other taxonomies. In such a manner, the analyst/designer can greatly influence the way that classifications of raw text are made. The preferred taxonomy is useful to influence the most appropriate interpretation of the taxonomy. Stated differently, there often are multiple ways to interpret a taxonomy. The preferred taxonomy gives the analyst the latitude as to how the interpretation is most appropriately made. Figure 8.6 shows that one taxonomy has been designated as the preferred taxonomy.

Figure 8.6 One taxonomy has been designated the preferred taxonomy

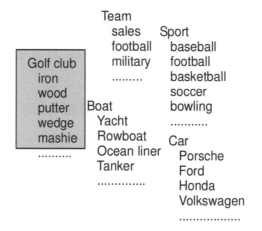

External Categorization

An important aspect of processing text is managing external categorization. External categorization is handled by managing text through classifications based on taxonomies. If you are going to be doing external category processing, then you will need taxonomies. But if you are not going to be doing external category processing, you will not need taxonomies.

The term "external category" refers to the fact that the contents of a body of text are analyzed in accordance with externally created criteria. Figure 8.7 shows that several external criteria, that is, taxonomies, are selected and that those criteria are applied against a body of text.

Figure 8.7 Applying taxonomies to a body of text

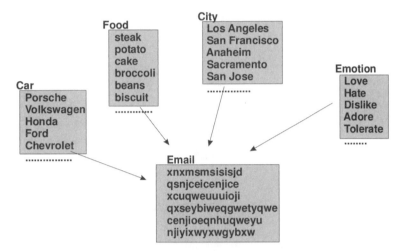

For example, the body of text may be some emails and the external criteria may be business terms. In this case, after applying the external criteria to the contents of an email, there may be text in the email that refers to business-relevant terms. Or there may be emails where the contents have no intersection with any business term. The criteria that are chosen are strictly external to the contents of the document or documents being analyzed.

Real World Problems

In truth, the taxonomy found in Figure 8.2 is a deceptively simple taxonomy. You will find the complexities discussed in this section in most unstructured data warehouse projects.

HIERARCHIES WITHIN THE TAXONOMY

It is completely normal to have a hierarchy of data buried within the taxonomy. In Figure 8.8 it is seen that there is a hierarchy of cars. The hierarchy has a first level of sports car, hybrid car, utility car, and SUV. Then, within the first level of categorization, there is another level of categorization – a sports car may be a Porsche or a Ferrari.

Figure 8.8 Hierarchies within a taxonomy

```
Car
   sports car
      Porsche
      Ferrari
      Lotus
   hybrid
      Honda
      Toyota
   utility
      Hummer
      Jeep
   suv
      Chevrolet
      Ford
      Dodge
```

Indeed, this creation of a hierarchy within a taxonomy can (and usually does) go much further than the two levels of hierarchy that are shown in Figure 8.8.

There is an important implication when considering the levels of hierarchy that are contained in a taxonomy. That consideration is the number of different levels of hierarchy within the taxonomy which open the doors to complexity.

MULTIPLE TYPES WITHIN THE TAXONOMY

As an example of the sort of complexity that can arise when dealing with a real-world taxonomy, consider that with multiple levels of hierarchy in a taxonomy, it is possible to have different types in the taxonomy. For example, the taxonomy for "Car" may have cars "typed" by car type: sports, utility, and so forth. But it is also possible to have cars categorized by cost: expensive, less expensive cars. Or it is possible to have cars "typed" by weight. In fact, cars may be categorized many different ways. And of course, the same car can be found in many different categories.

RECURSION WITHIN THE TAXONOMY

Another complicating factor is that with the permutations that can arise, there is the possibility of recursion. Recursion occurs when one element in a hierarchical structure directly or indirectly refers to itself. The analysis done following a recursive structure becomes complicated because the system has to "remember" what has already been processed in order to not reprocess that same element. It is entirely possible for a recursive analytical process to get caught in an infinite loop.

For example, a jeep may be a form of utility vehicle. A utility vehicle may be a form of off road vehicle. And a type of off road vehicle may be a jeep. Unless the analyst is careful, it is possible to execute a subroutine that never finishes execution when examining this relationship.

RELATIONSHIPS BETWEEN TAXONOMIES

An interesting relationship that frequently occurs with taxonomies is the relationship wherein one of the items in one taxonomy has a direct or strong relationship with an item in another taxonomy. Figure 8.9 shows such a relationship.

Figure 8.9 A relationship between two taxonomies

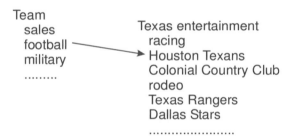

When there are many cross-relationships between taxonomies, the analyst/designer needs to consider whether or not another categorization would better fit the needs of classifying and categorizing the raw text that is to be processed.

Taxonomies and Data Modeling

In many ways, taxonomies are the equivalent of data modeling for structured text. Stated differently, taxonomies are to unstructured text what data models are to structured data. Taxonomies represent an abstraction of unstructured text just like a data model represents an abstraction of structured data.

It may strike you that if there are many taxonomies, and if the taxonomies are built externally, then it probably does not make sense for an organization to model and build something that already exists. Indeed, there are rich sources of taxonomies that are already built and are available for supporting Textual ETL. There are some major advantages to acquiring a taxonomy that has already been built:

- You don't have to spend the resources to build it yourself
- Commercially built taxonomies are created by subject matter experts and are probably more robust and more accurate than those you could create
- If it has been built externally, it doesn't have to be maintained manually
- If it has been built commercially, it probably is available in multiple languages.

There are, then, some very good reasons for using commercially built taxonomies. However they are acquired, taxonomies are the key to being able to categorize data in the Textual ETL process.

Key Points

- Taxonomies are nothing more than lists of categories or synonyms. The text is read, and if a word fits within a taxonomy, the category or synonym is added to the text. In doing so, analysis at the category level becomes a possibility.

- By breaking down the taxonomy into a series of parent/child relationships, the analyst/designer can simplify the taxonomy and make it fit for processing for the Textual ETL software.

- One taxonomy may be designated as the "preferred" taxonomy – the one to be used before any other taxonomy is used in the resolution of text. Only after a matching effort against the preferred taxonomy is complete is a matching effort attempted against the other taxonomies.

- External categorization is handled by managing text through classifications based on taxonomies. If you are going to be doing external category processing, then you will need taxonomies.

- In most taxonomies, you will often see the complexities of hierarchies, multiple types, recursion, and inter-taxonomy relationships.

- Taxonomies are to unstructured text what data models are to structured data.

CHAPTER 9
Coping with Large Amounts of Data

There are many ways that the architecture of the unstructured data warehouse is measured. One of the most important ways that success is measured is in terms of the ability of the architecture to manage large volumes of data.

If there is one hallmark of unstructured data, it is the volume of data that can collect in an unstructured data warehouse. In the average corporation, there is far more unstructured data than there is structured, transaction-based data.

According to industry estimates, there is approximately 4 to 5 times the amount of unstructured data compared to structured data in the average corporation. Given that structured data has led to large data warehouses, it follows that unstructured data can lead to *really* large data warehouses.

So what are the problems associated with really large data warehouses? There are many problems associated with the collection and management of large amounts of data. Some of the problems are:

- **Access time**. The larger the amount of data, the slower the response time. Even with indexing and with data warehouse appliances, very large amounts of data entail longer response time. And the larger the data grows, the worse response time gets.
- **Cost**. Even though the unit cost of storage continues to get cheaper, the rate of growth of data exceeds the rate of decline in the cost of storage. Increasingly, the cost of storage relates more to the infrastructure to manage the storage than it does to the unit cost of storage, and the infrastructure cost of storage increases as the volume of storage being managed increases.
- **Manageability**. Simply stated, small amounts of data are manageable and large amounts of data become unwieldy to manage. Simple tasks such as creating an index, loading data,

153

doing a summarization, and so forth, all become difficult or awkward in the face of large volumes of data.

- **Coexistence with structured data in the same data warehouse.** It is very possible for the volume of unstructured data in a data warehouse to completely overwhelm the volume of structured data in a data warehouse. This can make it challenging (or impossible) to efficiently access and analyze the structured information in the warehouse.

There are, then, some very good reasons to approach the volumes of data found in the unstructured data warehouse environment carefully. Throughout the building and loading of data into the unstructured data warehouse, there must be constant vigilance for the volumes of data that are being accumulated, and an insistence on reducing unnecessary and unneeded unstructured data wherever possible.

The following are some of the more important techniques and approaches to the management of the volumes of data that occur in the unstructured data warehouse. In some cases, one approach may not apply, but all of the approaches should always be considered.

Keeping Unstructured Data in Place

The primary architectural consideration of managing large volumes of text in an unstructured data warehouse is that of not placing actual text in the unstructured data warehouse. Instead, the text that is placed in the unstructured data warehouse is that text that is most useful in decision making. Stated differently, the unstructured data warehouse should contain only the distilled data that is useful for decision making, while the actual text remains at its source.

As a simple example, suppose there was this email:

> I received your invoice for $238.18 yesterday. I will see to it that AM Rogers is paid posthaste. Thank you for the opportunity to do business with you.
>
> Todd Beltham

The email would remain in its original state on a server. Only certain data would be placed in the unstructured data warehouse. The values "invoice", "$238.18", "AM Rogers", and "Todd Beltham" would be placed in the unstructured data warehouse. In doing so, there is much less actual text found in the unstructured data warehouse than there is in the server holding the emails. But the data found in the data warehouse is still useful for decision making purposes. Figure 9.1 shows the division of the bulk of the data and the data needed for decision support processing.

Figure 9.1 Only a small subset of unstructured data is placed in the data warehouse

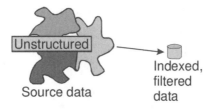

The strategy of dividing the textual data into two places: the original storage location and an unstructured data warehouse – is fundamental to the management of the volume of data found in the

Implementing Backward Pointers

It goes without saying that once decision support processing is performed against the data found in the unstructured data warehouse, if there is a need to go to the server on which the actual source of the data resides (such as an email), such a traversal should be natural and easy. The unstructured data warehouse contains a pointer (or multiple pointers) to the actual data on the server. Figure 9.2 shows that the unstructured data warehouse contains one or more pointers back to the source data.

Figure 9.2 The unstructured data warehouse points to the actual data

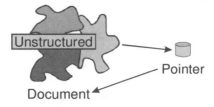

The strategy of dividing the textual data into two places: the original storage location and an unstructured data warehouse – is fundamental to the management of the volume of data found in the

textual unstructured environment. The example used to illustrate this point is an email; of course other kinds of textual data also follow this example.

Doing Iterative Development

A second approach to the handling of large volumes of data is to use the iterative, step at a time, approach in the editing, loading, and handling of data. The importance of iteration has been emphasized several times in this book. There are many reasons why doing processing in an iterative manner makes sense. The main reason why it makes sense is that rework is usually the norm for processing text. It is unusual to specify a process and have the process operate as expected the first time (or even the second time). When handling text, rework should be a common, normal expectation because much of the handling of text is an art, not a science. Text is imperfect and therefore handling text is also imperfect.

Knowing that rework is a normal expectation, it just doesn't make sense to process large amounts of text at one time. In the face of large amounts of text, the most effective process is to tackle a small part of the text, then tackle the next small part of text, and so forth. Iterative processing, then, as seen in Figure 9.3, is the proper way to approach most processing that occurs in the textual data warehouse environment.

Figure 9.3 Iterative processing is essential

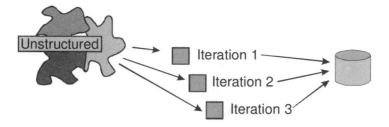

In order to do iterative processing efficiently and seamlessly, the output of each iteration must be compatible with every other iteration of processing. The alignment must be both structural and semantic. By making all the different iterations of processing compatible, the analyst/designer assures that the results of processing can be combined into a single, unified result after-the-fact.

Stated differently, if the results of each iteration of processing were not semantically and structurally compatible with every other result, the final product could not be created by merely merging the iterative results together.

Avoiding Rework

Another feature of Textual ETL processing is once data has been created, other data can be created incrementally, without having to redo work that has already been done. For example, suppose that an organization has created a document fractured index. It is possible to create a named value index without having to recreate the document fractured index.

Or suppose that an external categorization has been created for taxonomies ABC, BCD, and CDE. Then suppose that it is decided to produce an external categorization for taxonomy XYZ. The building of the taxonomy for XYZ in no way affects the validity or existence of the external categorizations built for ABC, BCD, and CDE.

With Textual ETL, the indexes can be extended or altered with no affect on the work that was done previously. The reason why this is important to the management of large volumes of data is that in most cases, massive amounts of rework are not necessary, or desirable. In the long run, this saves on the resources needed to manage large amounts of data.

Screening Data

Perhaps the most effective way of managing large amounts of data in the unstructured data warehouse environment is that of preventing unnecessary and unneeded data from ever getting into the unstructured data warehouse. On the one hand, it is true that the unstructured environment contains a lot more data than the structured environment. On the other hand, not all of that unstructured data belongs in the unstructured data warehouse. For example, suppose there are a lot of emails. The relevant sections of some emails undoubtedly belong in the unstructured data warehouse, but other emails do not belong there. Therefore, one of the processes that emails pass through before being sent to Textual ETL is a relevancy filter. Only those emails that have business relevance find their way into the unstructured data warehouse.

In doing so, a large percentage of the emails of a corporation never take up space and resources. By removing non business relevant emails, the volume of the data that finds its way into the unstructured data warehouse is limited. The technique of removing non business relevant data from the unstructured data warehouse is applicable to many other forms of unstructured data besides email. Figure 9.4 shows the filtering of data from the unstructured environment before the data is ever moved into the data warehouse.

Figure 9.4 Filtering of data is essential prior to loading into the data warehouse

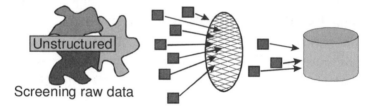

Removing Extraneous Data

In the same vein as filtering data comes the practice of removing extraneous data from the unstructured data warehouse. An example of the removal of extraneous data from the unstructured data warehouse is the removal of stop words from the data that is passed through Textual ETL. Stop words simply get in the way and add nothing to the analytical capabilities of the analyst/designer. Therefore, removing extraneous data from the unstructured environment is yet another way that the volume of data can be managed in the unstructured data warehouse environment. Figure 9.5 shows that extraneous data should be prevented from entering the unstructured data warehouse.

Figure 9.5 Removing extraneous data

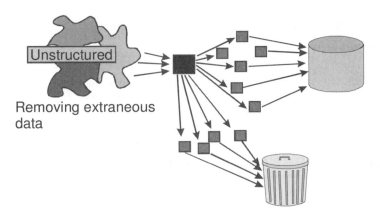

Selecting Appropriate Index Types
===

Another approach to managing the volume of data that comes with unstructured data is selecting the most effective index types. Recall Chapter 4, where we discussed each type of index. Simple indexes take up less space than fractured indexes. Named value indexes take up less space than simple indexes (in general). Making an index a sub doc index takes more time and space than the creation of a non sub doc index, and so forth.

Choosing the correct index type can go a long way towards managing space in the unstructured data warehouse environment. Of course, not all indexes can be created based on the source data, and not all indexes are useful to the end user. The analyst/designer must balance the effectiveness of the index versus the space the index will consume. In some cases, only a fractured index will suffice. If that is the case, then of course a fractured index should be built. But the analyst/designer should not automatically assume that a fractured index should always be built.

Figure 9.6 shows that there are many choices and the analyst/designer needs to be judicious in choosing the most appropriate type of index (or indexes) that will be built and placed in the unstructured data warehouse.

Figure 9.6 Choose the most appropriate type of index (or indexes)

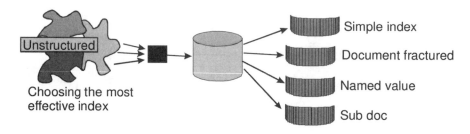

Parallelizing the Workload

Whenever large volumes of data are encountered, it is always an advantage to be able to process the workload in parallel. By processing the workload in parallel, the total elapsed time for processing is reduced. If n units of work need to be done and there are m processors, then the elapsed time required to do the processing is approximately n/m. (The n/m factor depends on being able to divide the workload evenly among the processors.)

Given that the results of Textual ETL processing are compatible, it is then easy to divide the input that needs to be processed into roughly separate and equal workloads and to use separate processors to operate on the workload. Of course, a parallel architecture can be used for this processing, but it is not necessary to use one. The parallelization of the workload can easily be done using physically and logically separate servers. Figure 9.7 shows the ability of textual ETL to process the workload in a parallel manner.

Figure 9.7 Ideally textual ETL should be processed in parallel

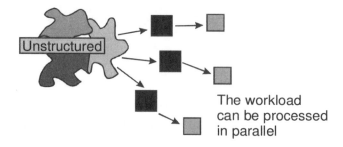

Building Small Logically Related Tables

When one looks at the unstructured data warehouse, it is easy to draw the conclusion that the unstructured data warehouse is a single large table. Such is not the case at all. The unstructured data warehouse is a collection of separate tables. The separate physical tables are logically (and loosely) connected. The physical separation of the tables is greatly advantageous in the face of large volumes of data. When tables are physically divided, they can be managed separately. Back up, loading, and even searching can be done individually. By having many separate physical tables:

- The work done against any one table can be done quickly
- The work done against all tables can be done in parallel
- The work done against any one table can be done in isolation from all other tables.

In other words, the physical structure of the unstructured data warehouse lends itself to being managed over a very large volume of data.

The logical structuring of data found in the unstructured data warehouse is often loose and informal. For example, there might be three tables that were created in 2003. The tables are logically related in that they apply only to events that occurred in 2003. There seldom are any formal, disciplined relationships created across the different physical tables that make up the unstructured data warehouse. Another example, what appears to be one customer table may be physically made up of a customer table for 2004, 2005, 2006, and so forth.

Dividing Data into Sectors

A final strategic, architectural consideration for managing the volumes of data in the unstructured data warehouse is that of arranging indexes into two "sectors". One sector is the primary sector. Data found in the primary sector is data that is easily and readily available to the end user for analysis. Data found in the secondary sector can be accessed, but must first be queued up for processing. By dividing data into two sectors, primary and secondary (or active and passive), the analyst/designer can ensure that when analysis is performed, it is done only against the data that is of most interest. Stated differently, when data is all grouped together and analysis is done against it, it is likely that many machine cycles will be spent looking at data that is not really relevant. In order to optimize the search experience for the end user, dividing tables of data into two classes optimizes the chances that the most effective analysis will be done for the fewest machine cycles.

Figure 9.8 shows that the ultimate tables for the unstructured data warehouse can be divided into two classes, and that the division of data into these two classes enhances the chances that the end user will be able to get to the most important, most useful data the quickest.

Figure 9.8 Two classes of unstructured data

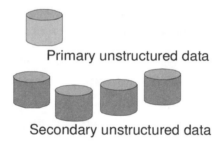

Primary unstructured data

Secondary unstructured data

Key Points

- Access time, cost, manageability, and coexistence with structured data are some of the many problems associated with really large data warehouses.

- The unstructured data warehouse contains only the distilled data that is useful for decision making while the actual text remains at its source.

- The unstructured data warehouse should contain a pointer (or multiple pointers) to the actual data on the server.

- Use an iterative, step at a time, approach in the editing, loading, and handling of data.

- Choose the correct index type for smart space management in the unstructured data warehouse environment.

- Whenever large volumes of data are encountered, it is always an advantage to be able to process the workload in parallel.

- Use multiple database tables to improve the efficiency of backing up, loading, and searching.

Processing data from a data warehouse perspective has always been a challenge, due to the volume of data (both input and in the data warehouse), the type of data, performance issues with disks and servers, and metadata issues. These challenges will be very relevant to unstructured data processing in the data warehouse environment, but there are some key changes in the way these challenges manifest themselves. This chapter will be focusing on the challenges and some technology choices that are suitable to unstructured data processing.

Unstructured data cannot be processed by regular Extract, Transform, Load (ETL) / Extract, Load, Transform (ELT) / Changed Data Capture (CDC) tools, therefore we need to use a textual ETL tool. The reason for this is the data that is processed is not structured in nature and requires significant effort in parsing, context analysis, and metadata tagging to be input into the storage structures in the data warehouse. In the following section you will learn more about unstructured data processing.

Processing Structured Data

Before we look at the unstructured database and how to architect it, let us take a quick look at normal data warehouse processing. To build a classical data warehouse, we normally process structured data through an ETL process, store the result set as tables and columns, classifying the relationships between the different elements with a relational model and a system of keys. This is a very straightforward process and can be simplified into manageable components. Traditional ETL tools, and more recently, CDC and ELT technologies, have made near real time capture of structured data and its subsequent processing into the data warehouse more achievable.

Structured data processing is governed by the following principles:

- **Business Requirements**. A finite set of business problems and the associated data required to be analyzed and reported or measured is what drives the need for a data warehouse or a datamart.
- **Data Model**. The data warehouse is built around the data model, which is driven by business requirements for how the business views and consumes data.
- **Level of Granularity**. Across the data warehouse, data can be stored at different levels of information. The associated hierarchies and calculations play a large role in determining the transactional nature of the overall system design.
- **Transformation**. Data is transformed from transactional to business entities and metrics and measures are applied to them. Master Data Management techniques (MDM) may be used when data is transformed to achieve conformance and standards of definition (although most companies did build conformed dimensions before MDM came into being). Business rules for transforming data are captured in ETL or CDC code and enforced on the data being transformed. The transformation of data is very data-centric because it involves transactional data, which is very structured in nature, and deals with products, locations, services, finances, and measures around these areas.
- **Metadata**. Metadata is the most often overlooked and understated component in data warehousing. It is a complex subject where most of the complexity lies in articulation, not in the implementation.
- **Data Security**. There are specific data privacy and security requirements that mandate how the data is acquired, transformed, and stored at rest. These requirements have evolved into industry-wide standards and there are several solutions built around them.

In retrospect, the processing of structured data into the data warehouse is finite and well-defined from a business or IT perspective. Let us look at the performance drivers of a data warehouse.

DATA WAREHOUSE PERFORMANCE

There are several key performance drivers for a data warehouse. The drivers of performance include the following:

- Data Volume
- Data Complexity
- User Volume
- User Complexity
- Real-Time Data Integration
- Data Latencies – Inbound and Outbound.

The primary challenges in Data Warehousing today are in the areas of:

- **Data Loading**. Loading data into the data warehouse is one of the longest processes. It is primarily controlled by the volume of data, the complexity of transformations, and the workload on the database at a given point in time. The many reasons for this have been discussed in depth in various ETL articles and case studies. To summarize, the process of extracting various data feeds, processing them through data quality and data profiling, and loading them with or without transformations to a final destination is time consuming, especially when the input volumes are low, there are smaller bursts of data, and the speed is impacted by the volume of data in the data warehouse.
- **Data Availability**. Data Availability Service Level Agreements (SLAs) have a profound impact on the need to have a high performance environment. For data to be pristine, integrated, and available for downstream applications like reporting and analytics, end user needs must be clearly documented. An additional aspect on which organizations often fall short, are data growth projections, data demand projections, and data retention cycles and associated SLA's that have not been documented.
- **Data Volume**. Within organizations, data volume in the data warehouse has been exploding. The reasons for this data volume explosion are:

o Compliance Rules such as Sox, HIPAA, Basel II, PCI
o New types of data including clickstream, web applications, blogs, forums, discussion threads, and competitive intelligence
o User adoption of BI, resulting in integration of applications and data from transactional and operational systems
o Longer storage of historical data in the data warehouse.

- **User Access**. Data access and availability are key components that lead to adoption of BI in any organization. In today's world, the business relies on data warehousing to help them make informed decisions, which means that users need to have access to the latest data in a timely fashion. This implies that data will need to be available for operational and analytical requirements with minimal latency from the time any event occurs in an organization's transactional systems. This data freshness will encourage users to seek the data warehouse platform for access to all data.

- **Storage Performance**. Disk and storage systems have been consistently improving over the years both in terms of speed and performance, while costs have been relatively stable and have, in fact, become less expensive. Architecturally, storage is shared by all areas of a data warehouse, making it a highly constrained area in terms of availability and performance. ETL and BI queries are not small traffic in nature, and consume a lot of space and network bandwidth. If multiple such queries are fired off on this shared storage architecture, even the best in class hardware and disk are not going to enable faster query processing and a lightning response time for results sets. Having said this, if we add mixed query workloads on the storage architecture, we are going to start seeing slower and slower performance cycles, resulting in poor query performance and a highly constrained network in terms of bandwidth. Even continued strides in improving the overall storage performance will not make it more optimal for data warehousing. Faster is Better does not fit in this space.

- **Operational Costs**. The operational cost of running and maintaining a data warehouse has been monumental in many organizations. Especially with the granularity of the data growing deeper and the need to store a greater amount of history, a two way explosion has resulted in an unmanageable amount of information to be handled by the data warehouse. Added to these exploding volumes are multiple kinds of related activities like data mining, predictive and heuristics analysis, which have placed a heavy demand on the resources both in hardware and in IT administration (DBA, System Administrator, Network Administrator roles).

Processing Unstructured Data

In the preceding section, we looked in-depth at the processing of structured data and its associated challenges. Let us now look at the challenges with processing unstructured data, which can be classified into Data, Acquisition, Processing, Storage, Integration, Usage, Volume, and Workload:

- **Data.** Data needs to be processed from acquisition to integration in the unstructured data world as much as we do in the structured data world.
- **Acquisition**. Data, in terms of the unstructured world, can be sourced from microblogs (like twitter), documents, emails, manuals, notes, speech to text, video to text, and much more. Based on the source of the data, there will be data quality issues arising from conversions of various formats, languages, phonetics, and grammar. The acquisition challenge is further divided into:
    - o **Digital text**. This is data typically found in documents, spreadsheets, and notes. The data is unstructured, formatted and available for processing with minimal data quality errors.
    - o **Email text**. This is data extracted from corporate and non-corporate emails. Classified as semi-structured data, there is some embedded master data and

metadata in the document. Data quality and grammar may be not at 100% accuracy.

- o **OCR text**. This is data from scanned material. The data is both unstructured and semi-structured, data quality is very poor, and sometimes transcription errors can cause context sensitivity issues.
- o **Speech to text**. This is data extracted from speech to text. Context and data quality due to accent can cause processing errors.
- o **Video to text**. This is data extracted from video to text. The processing issues are similar to Speech to Text conversion.

- **Processing**. Textual data is very verbose and can be processed multiple times to extract all the required information. For example – A patient's medical record can be dealing with both cardiology and diabetes in the same chat, but it needs to be processed based on the context of what information is being sought.
- **Storage**. The actual content of the textual data that is extracted for integration into an existing data warehouse or to build a new unstructured database, will be small in size and can be stored easily. The actual document that is processed will also need to be stored either online or offline.
- **Integration**. The text data that is extracted from different sources will need to be integrated into the data warehouse or other databases. This will require metadata on both the structured and unstructured data to be precise and ready for integration and usage.
- **Usage**. Data from textual ETL will be used by different users, and will mean different things to different users. The actual usage of the data will depend on its integration within the databases and the availability of metadata.
- **Volume**. The volume of data to be processed can be 140 words to 10MB and more. This means unpredictable performance when you take into consideration all the activities that textual ETL will perform:
  - o **Categorization**. This is the process of consolidating text into different categories for processing. For

example, you cannot mix legal documents with medical documents for processing.

o **Classification**. This is the process of classifying data into subject or context areas. For example, we need to sort out customer feedback on services in a store versus services provided online for the same product as different customer experiences and sentiments.

o **Context Tag**. Tagging is one of the fundamental processes in processing verbose text. This provides the ability to identify to which particular context a document matched. Remember, multiple categories can match a context and also the same document can match multiple contexts.

o **Matching**. This is the process of matching the associated metadata between structured and unstructured texts.

- **Workload**. Processing unstructured data deals with the problem of mixed workload processing. The workload depends on the following key factors:

o **Complexity**. The complexity of the data being processed including the actual size of each file, the number of files, the language, content, and taxonomies. The language that is being processed, for example English verse Portuguese verse Mandarin Chinese, can have varying degrees of complexities when being processed in a Textual ETL process. Also the type of content being processed brings different degrees of workload. For example, processing a web forum sentiment verse processing a legal document. In the case of the former, language, context and sentiment are three main parameters, while in the latter case, jargon, sensitivity, relevance, and language all matter. And, there can be multiple contexts for which processing have to done for the same document in multiple iterations. Thus content can drive processing times. A semantic hierarchy which can guide end user analysis is aided with the usage of taxonomies. While this method is very useful from a front end perspective, it adds workload when Textual ETL is being processed. Taxonomies often serve a purpose of reference lookup while processing text.

- o **Type of data**. The type of data being processed impacts the workload on the servers. Broadly, there are two types of data: text and non text. Text is any document, email, or web content that is raw text. Here, the workload is in processing different types of text where there are multiple contexts, and each of those has varying degrees of relevance. For example when we process plain text, we capture data in certain patterns verse processing email, where we capture data in other patterns. Non text is audio or video. Processing non textual content brings a whole new set of complexities where we need to pre-process and convert the video or audio to text, then understand the content and context sensitivity, finally being ready to process this workload.

- o **Availability of database**. As with regular data warehouse processing, the unstructured database has to be available for concurrent processing, meaning both loading and querying will occur simultaneously.

- **Infrastructure**. Infrastructure includes the application server, database server, storage and network. In terms of server load, unstructured data processing is very CPU and Memory intensive. Server processing is also an insert only operation, meaning there is no modification of an existing record, even when a document is reprocessed. Storage can be online or offline. Online is the result data that will be stored in a database. Offline is the original document that was processed, which will be needed for reference purposes, when the result set needs to link to the original document. In terms of network impact, it is lighter than normal data warehouse impact since there is a lower volume of data moved between the application and database servers. However, the impact of moving the original files post processing across the network, and retrieving the same on demand for display or search purposes, does pose workload on the network, which is normal with the way the data is processed by search engines.

Visualizing the unstructured data will be through the use of search engines, heat maps and text analytics. From a technology perspective, for inbound data and outbound processing, we will require a high performance server and a very scalable data processing environment.

Traditional technologies in application server, databases, storage and network, can be deployed to process text data. However, there are new technologies that can be specifically utilized to process unstructured data, namely the data warehouse appliance. We will see in the next section how the data warehouse appliance can provide benefits to processing unstructured data to the data warehouse.

Data Warehouse Appliance

A data warehouse (DW) appliance is an integrated set of servers, storage, operating system, database and interconnect, specifically preconfigured and tuned for the rigors of data warehousing. What makes an appliance appealing? DW appliances offer an attractive price / performance value proposition and are frequently a fraction of the cost of traditional data warehouse solutions.

First generation data warehouse appliances were introduced in the late 1990s by Netezza. Today, the marketplace is seeing solutions from Oracle, HP, Microsoft, Teradata, AsterData, ParAccel, KickFire, Kognitio, Greenplum, Extremedata, Infobright, and other vendors.

All DW appliances have been built on the following basic principles:

- **Shared Nothing Architecture**. Simply stated, in this architecture CPU, memory, and disk storage are not shared. Instead, a set of CPU's, memory, and disk storage form a processing unit called a node or blade.
- **Commodity Hardware and Storage**. This refers to using generic brands of hardware and storage, thereby reducing overhead costs often added by vendors. Commodity vendors

also provide special configurations for a manufacturer to allow superior computing capabilities.

- **Open Source DBMS Platforms with Additional Features**. These are geared to manage and handle data warehouse workloads. Some appliances utilize "columnar databases", which are becoming popular for niche applications.

- **Open Source OS**. Linux or Android platform based systems, for example.

- **Massively Parallel Processing Engines**. This is the secret sauce that is improvised by each appliance vendor. This is the software module that becomes the brains behind the system and its computing capabilities.

- **Data Integration Tools**. Appliance vendors have embraced open source ETL and BI vendor stack for providing an integrated offering. Examples include Talend for ETL and Jaspersoft for BI reporting.

- **Workload Optimizers**. Another secret ingredient in the appliance is the workload manager, which directs how inbound and outbound data processing is handled.

- **System Management and Monitoring Tools**. These are standard tools that are provided to manage the system from an administrator perspective. Although appliances are self managing, self tuning, and can accomplish tasks like query tuning, performance governance, and storage management, this module provides to the end user a GUI for human interface with command and control capabilities.

APPLIANCE ARCHITECTURE

The fundamental difference in the data warehouse appliance architecture is the "shared nothing" concept. Figure 10.1 shows the appliance architecture from a conceptual perspective. There are subtle differences and nuances to each appliance.

Figure 10.1 Appliance architecture (conceptual)

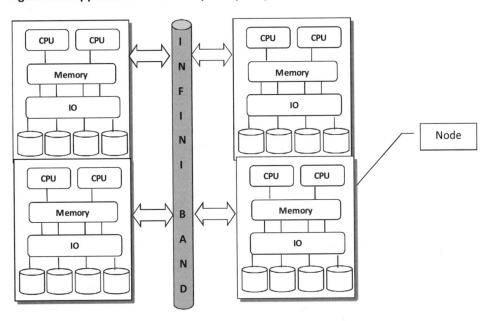

As seen in Figure 10.1, each node (or blade) of an appliance has its own set of CPUs, memory, IO channels, and storage. This self-contained unit is inter-connected by a switch called an "infini-band" switch. In a typical appliance, one node is designated as the "master" node. It will be responsible for coordination of workload management, data placement, data management, and user management.

The advantage of this architecture approach over a traditional three tier application server architecture, database server, and storage is:

- All storage is local to a particular node and can be managed by the node
- Data is typically distributed across two or more nodes. This helps in achieving workload balance, both on a single node and across nodes
- The IO is confined to one node and is managed by that node
- Should there be a failure in a node, workload switches to the remaining nodes in a seamless manner
- Should there be demand for more horsepower, one can simply add nodes and the system will add them to the infrastructure and scale the same, without external user intervention

- Nodes can be dedicated for loading, processing, and querying of data, thus enabling scaling of infrastructure with the type of workload.

DATA DISTRIBUTION

Figure 10.2 shows a typical data distribution across the data warehouse appliance.

Figure 10.2 Data distribution across the data warehouse appliance

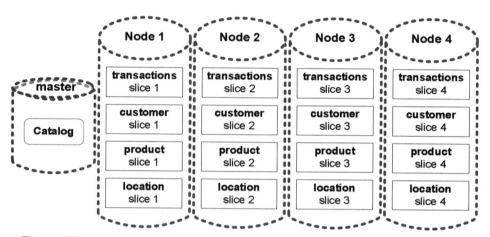

From Figure 10.2 we see that data is partitioned and distributed across multiple nodes. In addition to this, typically nodes 1 and 3 will mirror data slices and nodes 2 and 4 will mirror data slices. This brings in several advantages:

- **Fault tolerance**. Should a node fail, an alternate node can process the query.
- **Workload distribution**. Should there be a demand for the same data from a lot of users from a querying and analysis perspective, the system can be set up to distribute the load between multiple nodes.
- **Node balancing**. When additional nodes are added, they can be assigned to be automatically managed by the system, where the data is redistributed and the node workload is managed, or alternatively the node can be managed by an administrator and allocated to a specific task like loading or querying. (Note: This feature will vary from appliance to

appliance; the vendor can provide more detailed information in this regard).

WORKLOAD

Figure 10.3 shows the typical workload from a data warehouse perspective.

Figure 10.3 Typical workload from a data warehouse perspective

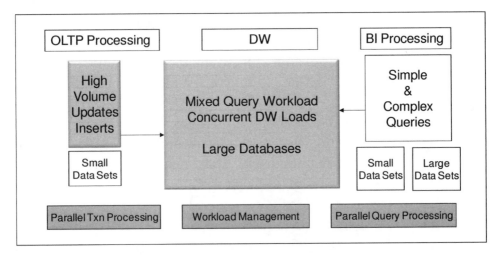

The inbound workload typically is transactional and discrete data sets in nature, while the outbound workload is a mix of small and large data sets, depending on the query that the user generates. The advantage of processing this workload in a data warehouse appliance is the ability to scale the resources on demand internal to the environment.

To recap, the benefits of the Data warehouse appliance are:

- **Integrated**. An integrated infrastructure stack to provide high powered computing platforms.
- **Self managing and tuning with minimal human intervention**. When using a regular RDBMS platform, a DBA needs to periodically tune the database and keep workload parameters balanced to manage the performance of the system. In the case of the Data Warehouse Appliance, there is no such specific activity to be executed across periods of time. The device is configured at setup time to be self

managing and tuning; an occasional tuning algorithm check will suffice.

- **Modular scalability**. Additional capacity can be added and scaled on demand. This is very similar to building a Lego block structure, where an additional node or blade is added to the Appliance and the system recognizes the new hardware and adds it to the available space and infrastructure. In some appliances, the system even does data redistribution based at the users request upon the addition to capacity.

- **Minimal footprint from a data center power and space consumption perspective**. Appliances are built to support the "go green" initiative; they consume minimal power and, due to radical improvements in hardware, most components today are capable of keeping the device from heating up. Due to the rack configuration, the hardware consumes less space, as it can hold more capacity than traditional hardware in a one box configuration.

- **Lower cost**. Provides lower capital expenditures (CAPEX) to the organization, since most companies buy capacity to grow into. And with highly efficient architectures in data and infrastructure, you can avoid expenses in hardware and software.

- **Reduced dependency on SQL**. With more application interface languages like Hadoop and MapReduce, there is a reduction in processing dependency on SQL while providing a lightweight footprint.

- **Quicker ROI**. When you deploy a data warehouse appliance, within the first two years of the deployment you will realize Return On Investment (ROI). In most organizations, the timeframe is shorter. There are a number of factors that influence this aspect, hence the exact timeframe of ROI is determined based on the needs. In the case of Unstructured Data Integration, which is leading to Customer Centric Improvements, the ROI realization is in months, not years.

BEST PRACTICES FOR IMPLEMENTING DATA WAREHOUSE APPLIANCES

Here are some best practices to help you make your data warehouse appliance implementation a success:

- **Determine your needs**. The first action item when implementing a data warehouse appliance is to determine your business requirements. This will drive the type of appliance platform that is needed, the applications that you can deploy on this platform, and the training that you will require from an IT and Business perspective.

- **Data Availability**. Determine the volume of data (Current and Historical), the types of data, the business requirements for data access, and availability from the time an event occurs in the organization.

- **Analytical Requirements**. Define requirements for OLAP, Analytics, and Multidimensional Cubes in terms of data. This will drive the types of data architecture, and platform selection will be easier.

- **Reporting Requirements**. Define the requirements for reporting applications and associated performance expectations.

- **Query Performance SLAs**. Define performance service level agreements for queries; classify queries by complexity, volume of data, and number of concurrent users.

- **Data Loading SLAs**. Define performance service level agreements for loading data; classify data by complexity in terms of transformations and volume of data.

- **Plan to minimize the data footprint**. By implementing a data warehouse appliance, reduce the data footprint in your infrastructure. This will require a data consolidation project to be implemented along with the data warehouse appliance implementation.

- **Solution Architecture**. Plan to optimize the different layers in your solution architecture when implementing an appliance. For example, in implementing a standalone solution with Netezza, you will plan for an optimization of queries. Similarly, when you implement AsterData, you will plan for optimizing ETL or Querying or both. The underlying architecture of an appliance will determine the ideal optimization that can be achieved.

- **Scalability**. All appliances have a "Lego" like scalability. Plan to add the additional space as required. This kind of planning will help you save initial and ongoing costs.

USING THE DATA WAREHOUSE APPLIANCE TO BUILD THE UNSTRUCTURED DATABASE

One of the better suited technologies to manage the integration of structured and unstructured data is the data warehouse appliance. The methodology to manage this integration is Inmon's Data Warehouse 2.0, recall Figure 3.1 copied here as Figure 10.4.

Figure 10.4 DW 2.0 environment

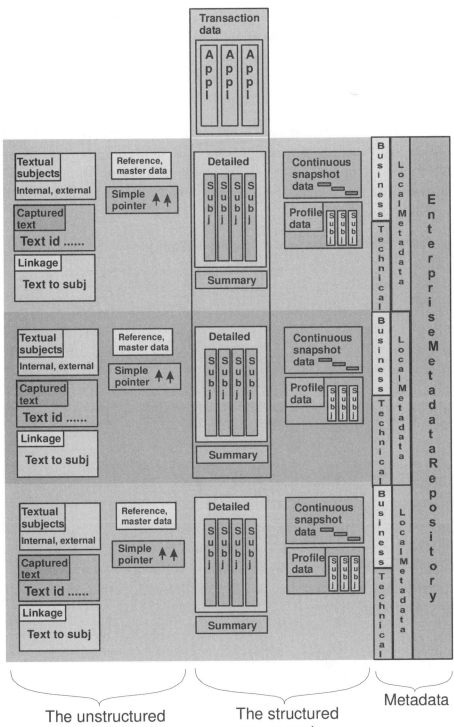

Using Data Warehouse (DW) 2.0, we can build an integrated data warehouse to store both the structured and unstructured data. We have discussed the data warehouse appliance in the preceding section; now we will see how it can handle the workload from an unstructured data processing perspective.

Figure 10.5 shows the typical workload from an unstructured data perspective. Inbound is discrete data with high volume inserts and outbound is a mixed workload of small and large search queries. Additionally, the search results will need to return the original document on demand.

Figure 10.5 Typical workload from an unstructured data perspective

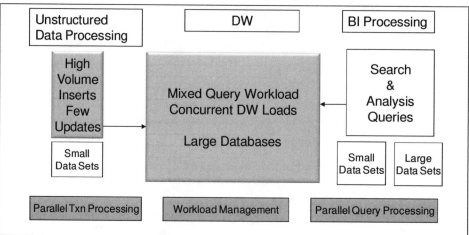

The overall technical architecture is shown in Figure 10.6. The key point to note here is that the workload on the input side will be managed by the Application Server and the workload on the output side will be managed by the Application Server and the data warehouse appliance.

Figure 10.6 Overall technical architecture

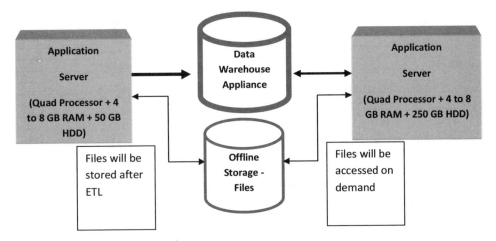

The technical architecture shown in Figure 10.6 presents the ideal setup for processing the unstructured database.

EXAMPLE OF PROCESSING UNSTRUCTURED DATA

A leading research institution has accumulated over 30 years worth of Doctors' notes and clinical trials on Pulmonary Critical Care (Heart/Lung). There are about 20,000 case notes, 100,000 clinical trials, and over 1,000,000 therapeutic notes and lab results. These notes were taken by many doctors from multiple specialties and multiple pharmaceutical companies.

Business Value

The institution was not able to use the data within these textual documents, since they were not available in a digital format; even if they were to be converted to a digital format, the data is verbose and not accessible. The business value was determined to be:

- Notes, case reports, and clinical trials can be very useful in current research and medical teaching.
- Data that is clear is the ability to predict the outcome of clinical trials, based on population clusters selected for such an exercise.
- Data collected over the years provides rich diagnosis options for nurses and critical care attendants.

- Medical taxonomy that has been gathered over the years can be utilized in guided search and is a very useful, content rich metadata.

Solution

The solution approach for this situation is as follows:

1. Identify the data to be processed
   - The files are stored across different technologies – Windows, DB2, VSAM, VAX
   - There are clinical trials and lab notes which are on paper
   - Some data lies in Excel spreadsheets
   - Some data lies in proprietary file formats
2. Data currently available
   - Master Data – Patients
   - Taxonomies
   - Metadata
3. Textual ETL Preparation
   - Convert the data to digital format; this includes OCR and Text conversion of data
   - Build the rules to process the data
4. Context
5. Spelling
6. Alternate Spelling
7. Homographs
8. Setup the taxonomies
9. Setup the data cleansing rules
10. Setup the iterations to process data
11. Process the data
12. Integrate the data
13. Post processing, integrate the text data results with the MDM, Metadata, and taxonomy data. Here the requirement to identify the context based result and its integration is a critical step to visualize the data.
14. Visualize the data, using techniques such as:

    o **Search**. We can use an integrated search engine to access the data from the result database and also the text document itself. A guided navigation engine can be custom deployed with a search interface. Some popular technologies include Endeca, Microsoft Fast, and Google.

- o **Self Organizing Maps (SOM)**. A heat map with subject based concentration, the SOM is a very useful visual tool when observing cluster based behaviors. A well known SOM engine is published by IDS.
- o **Geo-Spatial Maps**. When the data from clinical trials is visualized with an integration of Geographic tools, a time series based analysis and trending can be visualized using Geo-Spatial maps.

Technology Architecture

For a situation like the current discussion topic, the technology choices will be as follows:

- **Application Server**. 2 Quad-Core processor server, 8GB RAM, 250GB HDD
- **Database Server**. Any standard database server or data warehouse appliance
- **BI Server**. A server similar to the application server.

Conclusion

The data processing and mining of textual data provides business value. In a test situation, which was setup for the purpose of writing this book, we found the following

- The creation of the SOM required multiple iterations. Especially important in the treatment of the words were stop word processing, alternate spelling, and homograph resolution.
- The SOM quickly showed all the correlative factors to pulmonary and heart related syndromes.
- We can drill down using the SOM tool.
- It will take about 30 minutes to create a SOM.
- Some of the correlative factors uncovered in the SOM were well known; other factors were totally unknown. The factors that were discovered had been in the doctors' notes from the

beginning; it is only with the SOM's that they became apparent.

Key Points

- There are a wide range of technology choices that can be used to deploy unstructured data processing, depending on your budget, your data volumes, your need to integrate with structured data, and other factors.

- The processing of structured data into the data warehouse is finite and well-defined from a business or IT perspective.

- There are a number of challenges with processing unstructured data, which can be classified into Data, Acquisition, Processing, Storage, Integration, Usage, Volume, and Workload.

- A data warehouse (DW) appliance is an integrated set of servers, storage, operating system, database and interconnect, specifically preconfigured and tuned for the rigors of data warehousing.

- One of the better suited technologies to manage the integration of structured and unstructured data is the data warehouse appliance.

SECTION III
Unstructured Data Warehouse Case Studies

This section puts all of the previously discussed techniques and approaches in context through three case studies: the Ablatz Medical Group, the Eastern Hills Oil Company, and the Amber Oil Company.

CHAPTER 11
The Ablatz Medical Group

There is a medical group, Ablatz Medical Group, that has a series of hospitals, laboratories, and associated pharmacies on the West coast of the U.S. The affiliated hospitals and clinics are located in the Bay Area, Orange County, Oregon, and Washington. In addition, there are facilities in Phoenix and Las Vegas.

The Ablatz Group has both clinical needs for information and research needs, as well. Collectively, the hospitals and clinics service the needs of over 1,500,000 patients on an outpatient and inpatient basis. Abltaz prides itself on state of the art medicine. The equipment that Ablatz equips its hospitals and facilities with is the most modern and the most advanced.

Ablatz freely passes patients among its facilities for diagnosis and treatment. While regular family physician relationships are established and maintained by Ablatz, Ablatz also has specialists who are referred to by the family physicians working at Ablatz. In addition, Ablatz regularly receives referrals from other physicians on the West coast. Even though it doesn't happen regularly, Ablatz occasionally gets referrals from well outside the West coast, from places such as Mexico, the Orient, New York, Europe, and so forth.

In order to position itself in the medical community, Ablatz fosters research and publications. Many of the specialists at Ablatz work closely with medical facilities in the University environment, such as Stanford, the University of Oregon, and UCLA. Ablatz places a high premium on its doctors when they publish original research.

Information Systems

The medical information systems at Ablatz go back a long way. The very first records from Ablatz were recorded and organized on 3x5 cards and were stored in a set of wooden trays. Ablatz still keeps these records, more for showing to the public, than for actual usage. Ablatz has long gone away from 3x5 cards and wooden boxes because of the sheer number of records and the need to access and analyze those records regularly. But they keep some of the early records around as a curiosity and to show visitors the early origins of the information systems at Ablatz.

Over the years, the information systems of the Ablatz Medical Group have been collected in a variety of ways. In the earliest years, information was collected on magnetic tape files in what were called "master files". In these master files were found records of all sorts of interactions with the hospital. There were billing records, records of insurability, operation reports, emergency room reports, doctors visit reports, and so forth. The master file records consisted of COBOL defined fields. Most of the COBOL fields were fixed in meaning and physical characteristics. But one of the fields was a "comments" field. In the comments field were found many important observations. These observations were about the success of the procedure, the outcome of medication, diagnoses, and so forth. The comments field contained a wealth of information. However, the information that was contained is in the form of text. There was no structure to the information found in the comments field.

Over time, the Ablatz Medical Group shifted from the gathering of information in master files to the gathering of information based on treatment encounters. The information based on treatment encounters was gathered each time an individual went to the doctor's office or went into the hospital. Each treatment encounter generated a very variable amount and type of information. Some encounters were brief and contained only a doctor's remarks. Other encounters were long and drawn out. These encounters contained notes from many doctors and nurses. In addition, laboratory tests were included. In some cases, many laboratory tests were recorded.

In addition to making a record of each visit to the doctor's office or each visit to the hospital, these records were designed so that they could be strung together. For example, suppose that an individual made two visits to the doctor's office and three visits to the outpatient facilities of a hospital in the course of a year. The records of these visits to the hospital and the doctor's office could be "strung together", creating an annual record of the activities of the individual over the course of a year.

Special Treatment Collections

The Ablatz Medical Group also collects information another way. The Ablatz group has organized special treatment collections. These treatment collections are by disease. There are treatment collections for all major diseases that occur on a regular basis for the Ablatz Medical Group – diabetes, breast cancer, lung cancer, liver cancer, influenza, and so forth. These special treatment collections consist of the doctor's notes over the life of the treatment of a patient. Some of the doctor's notes are very short. Some of the doctor's notes are very extensive. The extent of the information about a patient depends on the life of the patient, the treatments, medications, tests, laboratory results, and procedures administered by the doctor. Some of the special treatment collections go back thirty or more years.

Other records of information collected and administered by the Ablatz Medical Group include billing information, insurance information, and Medicare information. The nature of this information is more financial than anything else.

Users

The information that has been gathered is used by a diverse group of people. Some of the information is used clinically to improve or manage the immediate health care needs of the patients being treated by the Ablatz staff of nurses, doctors, and other health care workers. Other users of the information include researchers, who analyze outcomes, effectiveness, and long term care. Yet other users are financial planners who manage the financial aspects of the Ablatz Medical Group. Still another group of users are people who manage the vendor relations with Ablatz. In short, there are a very diverse group of users of the information gathered at Ablatz.

The information is collected in a variety of ways. Some information is collected by admissions, as a patient enters the hospital. Other information is collected by the receptionist at the clinics and doctors' office. Other information is collected by means of tracking the activities of treatment: medications delivered, procedures completed, observations, laboratory tests, and so forth. Nurses enter some information, laboratory technicians enter other information, and doctors enter yet other information. In short, almost anyone involved in the day to day operations of Ablatz is capable of entering some of the information collected.

Some of the information collected by Ablatz is very structured. Hospital entry information, billing and insurance information, and a lot of laboratory results are of a very structured nature. But other information collected is of an unstructured variety. Doctors write their own shorthand for many interactions. Rarely are sentences written. And there are many abbreviations that are commonly used.

Some doctors use transcription services. Other doctors take notes (the old fashioned way.) And other doctors write on a screen. There is some degree of structure to the screen, but most of the information entered on the screen is essentially free form.

Integration

The need for integration of information is apparent and everyone is aware of the need. But most people have no idea where to start. Standard medical terminology is used wherever possible. But even with standardization of terms, there is still a need to a greater degree of integration. There are several factors that form a barrier to a high degree of integration:

- **HIPAA compliance**. Access to records limits who can see and access records. Because of this impediment, it is difficult to share or move data freely across the organization.
- **Textual foundation**. Much of the non financial information is in the form of text. Text does not lend itself to standardization in the world of databases.
- **Shorthand**. Doctors often use their own shorthand. This helps the doctors take notes, but forms difficulties when looking across the notes taken by multiple doctors.

- **Department autonomy**. Most departments look at the need for information only through the eyes of their department. Most departments do not perceive a need to look at information through the eyes of the organization.
- **Budget**. Departments have their own budget and are reluctant to spend money on a project that does not yield immediate and direct benefit to their department.
- **Vision**. Most departments simply are not interested in anything other than their own parochial interests. The fact that data in their domain has use outside of the domain is not of interest to the organization.
- **Focus**. Most departments view information as a secondary objective to the goals and success of the organization. Most organizations are much more interested in the immediate objectives of direct health care.

In truth, there are probably many more reasons why integration of information is not high on the list of the people and organizations in Ablatz Medical Group.

Unstructured Text

In order to start to address the problems of information in the medical/healthcare environment, it is decided to attack unstructured textual information. The hospital administrators have heard that Textual ETL can be done quickly and easily, unlike other forms of ETL and integrated processing.

The first thing the analysts and designers do is select a set of taxonomies. The taxonomies that are selected relate to the diseases, procedures, and medications that are commonly used in the hospital. Then the taxonomies are "weeded out". The weeding out process entails the removal of non useful words and phrases in the taxonomies. The taxonomies are weeded because the overhead of leaving non useful words in the taxonomy is great.

Next, a Textual ETL engine is selected. The Textual ETL engine is selected based on such capabilities as:

- Ability to handle lots of input sources
- Ability to create output in lots of formats
- Transformation capabilities
- Scalability
- Ability to merge outputs coming from multiple sources
- Ability to handle different languages
- Ability to integrate taxonomies.

Once the Textual ETL engine has been selected, a plan to integrate the many unstructured data sources found in the Ablatz environment is created. The first decision is to create a "card file" of all of the unstructured documents. The unstructured documents are read into the system and the metadata is stripped away from the documents. The source of the documents is captured in addition to the metadata. Once done, the index that is created contains a registry of all of the unstructured documents found in the Ablatz Medical Group.

The card catalog is useful for finding where a document is and determining what types of documents are in the medical group.

The next decision is to determine what kind of document libraries are to be created. It is decided to create three kinds of document libraries:

- A clinical library
- A research library
- A financial records library.

It is understood that of necessity, there will be overlap between the clinical and the research libraries.

Sources of Data

Once the basic libraries to be built are determined, the next step is to determine the likely sources of information for the different libraries. The likely sources are divided into different iterations. The plan is to process only a few documents of each type. The representative first documents are to be processed and reprocessed until the analyst is satisfied that the information produced by textual ETL is being produced properly. It is anticipated that it may take as many as ten iterations of the first few documents to process them properly. Once the first few documents are processed properly, then larger iterations of documents are processed. After each iteration of processing, the output is checked to make sure that the output contains the correct data in the proper format.

After one type of document is processed, another type of document will be processed using the same general plan. The general plan is outlined.

Next, the sources of the documents are determined. If any documents are paper based, the type of OCR that will be needed is determined. For simple paper input, where the font is standard and the strike of the print is strong, simple Adobe .pdf processing will suffice. For other types of paper documents, commercial OCR processing is required. The costs of OCR processing and the timing and volume of OCR processing is calculated and fed into the plan.

If any sources of documents that are electronically available are other than the standard sources, .doc, .docx, .pdf, .txt, then a plan must be made for entry of these document extension types into textual ETL. One plan is to read each document into a standard type such as Microsoft Word and adjust the document extension type into this standard type. Another plan is to find a utility on the Internet to create the needed extension type.

If the extension type that is to serve as input is Microsoft Excel (.xls), then there are several considerations. One alternative to just to read the entire spreadsheet in cell by cell and pluck out whatever data is needed and useful. A second alternative is to select only those cells that contain text. A third alternative is to select columns – either by column address or by column name and feed the columns in as input into Textual ETL. Another alternative for Excel is to select rows, either by row number or by selected text found in a row. And, of course, it is also possible to select a single cell from an Excel spreadsheet.

If the input type is Adobe .PDF, it must be determined whether to use a .PDF screen. On occasion, .PDF files can pick up an illegal character. Once an illegal character finds its way into processing, the program that is in execution dies upon reading it. Therefore, on occasion, if it is suspected that there may be illegal characters picked up by a .PDF, the usage of a .PDF screen is in order. When the .PDF screen is used, all illegal characters are replaced by blanks. Subsequent reads of the .PDF file do not then encounter an illegal character.

Once the input formats are aligned and the data is ready to be fed into textual ETL, the next step is to determine what kinds of indexes are to be produced. The types of indexes that can be produced are a function of the input and the processing that is desired after the input has been processed.

Determining what indexes are to be produced drives all subsequent processing. Stated differently, you cannot proceed with defining processing parameters for textual ETL unless you know what index types are to be produced.

Textual Operating Parameters

Now the processing parameters for Textual ETL are created. These parameters may include such things as:

- External categorizations
- Stop word processing
- Alternate spelling
- Homograph resolution
- Clustering
- Proximity analysis
- Pattern searching, and so forth.

Once the parameters are specified, the execution panel is prepared, the queue for processing is established, and processing commences. It is absolutely abnormal for the first setting of parameters to be correct. There are so many nuances to text and so many possibilities, that an accurate initial parametric setting is almost unheard of. Instead parameters are set, a few documents are run, the results are checked, the parameters are reset, the documents reprocessed, and so forth.

Once the parameters are set properly, the different iterations of documents are processed. At the end of each iteration, the results are stored, the work areas are cleared, and a new set of tables are created. The different sets of results are combined, and a consolidated database consisting of unstructured data cast in the form of a relational database is created.

In some cases, the running of textual ETL is a onetime process. In other cases, new text is constantly being entered and there is an ongoing need for the running of textual ETL.

In such a manner the textual component of information in the Ablatz Medical Group is created and integrated.

Visualization

There are other forms of textual ETL information in Ablatz. That form is the visualized form of text. The visualization of text occurs in the form of SOM's or "self organizing maps". The self organizing maps are also sometimes called "heat maps" because of their similarity to a heat map. The self organizing maps are good for looking at whole bodies of text and their correlative factors.

CHAPTER 12
The Eastern Hills Oil Company

The Eastern Hill Oil Company (EHOC) is an oil company that has been in business many years. As such, they have many contracts. When management is asked if they have information from their contracts, management always says "yes". But when questioned about what having contracts means, management states: "We go and find the contract. We then get one of our lawyers to read it. Then we can ask anything that we want."

And of course, if managing a contract means looking after one contract, then indeed EHOC does have control of their corporate contracts.

But EHOC has hundreds of thousands of contracts. And from the perspective of managing their corporate contracts as a whole, EHOC has no idea what is in their contracts. For example EHOC cannot answer such questions as:

- "What contracts are going to expire in six months?"
- "How many acres do we have under contract in Texas?"
- "How much liability is there for drilling damages in New Mexico?"
- "What total amount has been paid for contracts that are paid up leases?"

The fact of the matter is that when the body of contracts is considered, no one has any idea what is in the contracts. And that is because the contracts are in the form of text.

One day, an analyst from EHOC decides that there indeed is a wealth of information in corporate contracts. On this day, the analyst decides to build a database that can be analyzed based on the data found in the corporate contracts.

The analyst selects a tool that can do textual ETL. The analyst then sorts the contracts into general classifications; some contracts are pipeline contracts; some contracts are refining contracts; some contracts are distribution contracts; some contracts are oil and gas leases, and so forth. In all, there are many different classifications of contracts.

The next step the analyst goes though is to select a few representative contracts from one of the general classifications. The analyst then sorts through representative contracts and looks for the important information that stands out in each contract. In the case of oil and gas leases, the analyst selects the following indicative data:

- Lease number
- Lease date
- Lease termination date
- Lessor
- Lessee
- Well location
- Acreage under lease
- Distance from existing site
- Term amount
- Gas product type
- Drilling liability
- Pipeline easement
- Termination clause
- Minimum production requirement
- Well depth limitation.

Then the analyst takes each one of the terms and looks in the contract to determine delimiters for the term. Given the number of contracts, for nearly all terms, there are multiple sets of delimiters.

The analyst then creates a new document definition for the contract type in the textual ETL tool. And for each term that has been identified, the analyst creates an index specification. The index specification merely states that the document type is going to have an index associated with it. The analyst creates an index specification for each term.

Next, the analyst specifies the delimiters associated with the index. There are as many delimiters – beginning and ending – as there are unique ways of specifying the term. Now the document definition, the indexes that belong to the document, and the delimiters that apply to the document are specified.

The analyst then creates a panel that specifies that named value processing should take place. The analyst loads the queue with the first of the representative contracts. Now the analyst runs the textual ETL software against the contracts.

The first of the output is produced. Upon glancing at the output, the analyst finds that most of the terms that are desired to be indexed are, indeed, indexed. But there are several terms that are not found. The analyst makes a list of the terms which have not been found. The analyst then returns to the delimiter and index specifications. Then the analyst carefully and meticulously writes down what each delimiter is.

Next, the analyst returns to the contracts and examines the terms that should have been found but were not. The analyst compares the delimiter to the actual contract term and discovers what the actual delimiter specification should have been. The analyst returns to the textual ETL software and makes the necessary correction to the ETL software specification for delimiters.

The analyst reruns the Textual ETL software and recreates the indexes. The analyst once again examines what indexes have been produced by the software. If all of the indexes have been produced properly, the analyst is ready to run the full set of contracts through the system. If the indexes have not been successfully created by the Textual ETL software, the analyst readjusts the delimiters.

The process of setting and adjusting the delimiters continues until all the parameters have been properly set.

Once the parameters have been properly set, the analyst then runs all the contracts through the textual ETL process. If there are a lot of contracts to be processed, then the analyst breaks up the processing run into reasonable, smaller sets of contracts. If multiple iterations of processing have to be done, then the results of processing are consolidated into a single database.

Once all the contracts of a certain type have been processed, it is time to process another type of contract.

But before a new type of contract is processed, the parameters that have been established need to be saved. The analyst does not want to destroy the parameters because if there was ever a need to process more contracts of the same type, or if there is a need to reprocess existing contracts, then the analyst does not want to be faced with the problem of recreating the parameters.

In order to avoid having to recreate the parameters, the parameters are saved to a work area by the Move/Remove Utility. The first thing the Move/Remove Utility does is to move the parameters that have been established to a separate work location. Then the Move/Remove Utility cleans out whatever parameters there are in the Textual ETL parameter section so that a new set of parameters can be specified.

After the databases are created for the different contracts, the analyst takes the contract data that is on a database and allows Business Intelligence software to be used against the data. Now analytic processes show all sorts of information against the contracts that were impossible to calculate before.

CHAPTER 13
The Amber Oil Company

Amber Oil Company (AOC) has been in business for a number of years. AOC is a full service oil and gas explorer, pipeline, refinery, and distribution company. AOC explores for oil, mostly off shore. Upon discovering oil, the oil is shipped by pipeline to the storage facilities at one of several refineries. At the refinery, the crude is separated, refined, and turned into one of several oil products. Of course, the product that is most common is gasoline. But there are other byproducts of crude oil, as well.

Once converted, the gasoline is then stored and shipped to a network of filling stations. At the filling station, gasoline is sold to the consumer.

AOC, then, is both an upstream and downstream oil and gas producer.

The jobs that AOC has are not particularly safe. Accidents regularly occur in several places at AOC. Open water drilling platforms are not particularly safe places. Refineries are not particularly safe places. Occasionally there is an accident associated with pipelines. And even distribution is a place where accidents occur.

The accidents that occur are very varied. Some accidents are very common and are not particularly life threatening. As gas is being distributed in a delivery truck, there are occasionally traffic accidents. Most of these traffic accidents are of the "fender bender" variety and are normally not life threatening. Only once in a blue moon is there an accident at headquarters where back office work is done. And these accidents tend to be very non-life threatening.

On the other hand, there are accidents that occur in the refinery and on the ocean drilling platform that are very life threatening. Drilling for oil is always a dangerous proposition, and when the drilling occurs on an open water platform, the factors of danger are multiplied. Oil drilling platforms on the ocean are dangerous places. In addition, refineries are also dangerous places. There are dangerous chemicals in a refinery. The chemicals are often under a lot of pressure and the equipment found in a refinery can be dangerous. Because of these factors, there are genuinely life-threatening conditions in certain parts of AOC.

Safety is a constantly occurring theme at AOC. AOC very proactively promotes an awareness of safety for all of its workers. But safety is especially stressed in the more dangerous parts of AOC.

One of the practices that AOC has employed over the years is to create a daily log of all incidents that occur throughout the AOC environment. On a daily basis, all incidents worthy of notice are logged. The incidents that are logged include all accidents or near accidents, as well as other noteworthy news items relative to the successful running of AOC. The report is called the Incident Report, or the "IR".

AOC has been producing the IR for over a decade. Different parts of the organization report any incidents to an office at headquarters. The incidents are collected and are written into the IR. The IR is written in a paper and pencil format. The daily reports are bound together and placed in the corporate archives.

The kinds of incidents that are found in the IR include:

- Automobile accidents made in the delivery of gasoline
- Drilling accidents, where pipe is lost or improperly used
- Drops in pressure
- Pipeline leaks
- People falling from platforms
- Hurricane evacuations
- Loading accidents
- Over heating
- Over pressured equipment
- Equipment breakage
- Spillage
- Fires.

In short, any abnormal operation at the AOC facility is reported, including accidents.

The IR is used in many ways, such as:

- Insurance reviews
- Government safety reviews
- Management reviews
- Equipment usage and lifetime reviews.

One of the most important uses of the IR information is its value in a lawsuit. Should there be a lawsuit, the IR gives an immediate account of the incident. In addition, if a claim is made that there are unsafe conditions, the IR can be used to verify or negate such allegations. In short the organization has many uses for the information found in the IR report.

One day a computer analyst discovers the IR report. The analyst thinks that there are many useful pieces of information in the IR report that are not being used. The difficulties in analyzing the IR report are:

- The IR report is on paper
- The IR report is in the form of text.

The computer analyst declares that with modern technology, these obstacles can be easily overcome. The computer analyst begins by examining the font and strike of the paper that make up the IR report. The font is Arial and the strike appears to be strong. The analyst then reads the IR pages into an .Adobe .PDF format. Once in an Adobe .PDF format, the analyst then uses the Adobe OCR facility to capture the text inside of the .PDF.

The analyst looks at the results of the OCR capture inside Adobe and it appears that nearly all the words have been captured correctly. The analyst then procures a textual ETL tool and starts to examine the IR pages and to see what information there is to be captured.

The analyst decides to look at such things as:

- Where accidents have occurred
- What kind of accidents have occurred
- The time of day that accidents have occurred
- The day of the week that accidents have occurred

- The severity of the accident
- The dollar damage estimate that the accident has caused
- Whether or not the accident has disrupted the flow of oil and/or gasoline.

The analyst then looks for delimiter values that describe where the information can be found. Some of the information is easily delimited, while other information is not.

In addition the analyst looks for patterned variables. The analyst identifies the variables and identifies the unique pattern that defines each variable.

The next type of data the analyst specifies is numeric data that has been written in a textual format.

Once the proper parameters have been defined to the Textual ETL software, a few of the daily reports are processed through textual ETL. The analyst examines the database values that have been created and finds that several parametric specifications have not been made properly. The analyst compares the parametric specifications made to textual ETL versus the text as found in the daily reports, then adjusts the parameters and repeats the process of creating a database through textual ETL. This process continues until the analyst is satisfied that the correct data is being created in the database.

Now the analyst starts to run the daily reports through the textual ETL software, creating a database along the way. At the end of each run of the daily reports, the analyst stops to make sure that the correct values of data are being captured.

Soon, a year's worth of the daily reports have been passed through the Textual ETL process. The data that has resulted from passing through the Textual ETL software is consolidated into a single database in standard software such as Oracle.

At this point, the analyst starts to use a Business Intelligence tool to look at the data that has been gathered. The analyst examines the data that has been collected over a year's time and finds out such things as:

- Which locations in AOC are the most dangerous?
- What activities are the most dangerous?
- What time of day is the most dangerous?
- Which job position is at the most risk?
- Which equipment is the most dangerous?

By looking at all the incidents and accidents that have occurred, the analyst can start to detect patterns. The patterns that are detected are all relevant to enhancing safety at AOC. Now AOC can become proactive in elevating the safety of its employees.

Maximizing Search Engines

The Business intelligence systems of future will be minimally dependent on SQL based reporting and information retrieval. Instead the BI of future will be based on Semantic technologies where the metadata and the associated context will form the crux of search, information retrieval and reporting. For example if you are a business analyst at a large pizza chain, your query will be "Pizza's sold yesterday" rather than "Select count(*) from sales where date = 'dd/mm/yyyy'".

Before we examine how we can utilize a combination of technologies to progress to that realm of BI, we will examine how legacy search works and its shortcomings.

LEGACY SEARCH

Search engines use automated software programs to survey the Web and build their databases. Web documents are retrieved by these programs and analyzed. Data collected from each web page is added to the search engine index. When you enter a query at a search engine site, the input data is matched against the search engine's index of all the web pages it has analyzed. The best results are then returned to the user as hits, ranked in order with the best results at the top.

Legacy search depends on keyword searching. The most common form of text search on the Web, search engines do their text query and retrieval using keywords.

What is a keyword? It can simply be any word on a webpage. For example, if we use the word "complex" making it one of the keywords for a webpage in some search engine's index, you will get a myriad of hits on DW2.0. But in the same search if we use a word "junk", we might get useless hits and results.

What this means is, unless a document that is published on the web, has a specific set of keywords for the document (normally managed by metadata or meta tags), it's up to the search engine to determine keywords. Essentially, this means that search engines pull out key words and index words that appear to be significant based on certain rules. These rules are created by search algorithm developers for what words are usually important in a broad range of documents. The title of a page usually gives useful information about the subject of the page. Words that are mentioned towards the beginning and words that are repeated several times throughout the document are the most common keywords that are acquired for the document. Some search engines index every word on every page while some engines index only part of the document and in some cases for the same document.

The deficiencies with keyword searching include:

- Only a full-text indexing systems generally pick up every word in the text except commonly occurring stop words such as "a," "an," "the," "is," "and," "or". Stop word processing is not a full feature support across all search engines. Public search engines like Google or Bing might support it, in terms of enterprise search appliances, this is not a default.
- Keyword searches have a tough time distinguishing between words that are spelled the same way, but mean something different (hard rock can mean a popular café or can refer to a stone). This often results in hits that are completely irrelevant to your search input.

- Search engines also have a defect in not supporting stemming – that is, if you enter the word "move," should they return a hit on the word, "mov?" What about verb tenses that differ from the word entered by only an "s," or an "ed"?
- Search engines also cannot return hits on keywords that mean the same, but are not actually entered in your query. A query on heart attack would not return a document that used the word "cardiac" instead of "heart."
- Search engines cannot associate the context to the search, for example your search intention was to learn about heart attack and you have to sift through 1.5 million hits.
- Many, but not all search engines allow you to use so-called Boolean operators to refine your search. These are the logical terms AND, OR, NOT, and the so-called proximal locators, NEAR and FOLLOWED BY.

RELEVANCY RANKINGS

Search engines return results with page or relevancy rankings. They list the search result hits according to how closely the results match the search input. But the results leave users more perplexed and often frustrated.

Why does this happen? Most often search engines use the search terms frequency of occurrence within a document as a primary way of determining whether a document is relevant. If the search input is "colon cancer", and the word "colon" appears multiple times in a document, the search engine determines the document to be relevant to your search and positions it to near the top of the result list. If your keyword is a commonly used phrase or has multiple other meanings, we could end up with a lot of irrelevant hits. The more clearly relevant the results are, the more we're likely to adapt to the search engine.

The main issues of relevance and ranking have been addressed by Bing and Google in the recent year (2009-2010). But the deficiencies of keyword search and the ability to link context have not been clearly solved. This is due to multiple issues including the public domain, the volume of data and contextualization of the same.

Using an unstructured database, enterprises can leverage the ability to enhance their search beyond keywords and add more context and relevancy to documents that are sourced internally and externally to the organization.

By integrating the unstructured database along with Metadata and Meta-Tags, MDM and an enterprise search appliance, we can build an extended search engine. The advantage of an extended search appliance is the ability of an enterprise to use unstructured data in a way that has never been used before.

Significant examples of an extended search appliance can be:

- **Legal search appliance**. Lawyer offices can access volumes of case data, rules and interpretations in one search rather than sifting through hours of documents, which are more prone to human interpretation and also plausible error.
- **Nurse and Paramedical Management**. CCU and ICU units can leverage patient management reports, medical research data, patient therapy and treatment information in one search process. This will save precious time in managing patient trauma and provide the doctors an opportunity to treat the patient based on accurate symptoms than work through trauma. This will reduce risk of negligence and any associated medical and legal risks.
- **Maintenance and Safety**. We can prevent a future BP like explosion if we can integrate unstructured maintenance data along with safety reports, safety updates and safety management.

As you have read through this book and this chapter, you will realize that by building an effective unstructured database, we can improve BI and Search to the next level in many enterprises.

DAMA International 2009. *Data Management Body of Knowledge (DAMA-DMBOK)*, New Jersey: Technics Publications, LLC.

Hoberman, 2009. *Data Modeling Made Simple 2nd Edition*, New Jersey: Technics Publications, LLC.

Inmon W., 2005. *Building the Data Warehouse 4th Edition*. New York: Wiley.

Inmon W., Nesavich A. 2008. *Tapping into Unstructured Data*. Boston, MA: Prentice Hall.

Maydanchik, A. 2007. *Data Quality Assessment*. New Jersey: Technics Publications, LLC.

Mosley, M. 2005. *DAMA Dictionary of Data Management*. New Jersey: Technics Publications, LLC.

abstraction, 83

alternate spelling, 83

alternate spelling index. *See* index, alternate spelling

articles, 23, 70, 111

BI. *See* Business Intelligence

blather, 28–29, 37, 135

Business Intelligence, 36, 76, 77, 202, 206

business requirements, 101, 166

card catalog, 112, 120

case, 79

case study

    Ablatz Medical Group, 189–97

    Amber Oil Company, 203–10

    Eastern Hill Oil Company, 199–202

CDC. *See* Changed Data Capture

Changed Data Capture, 165

checkpoint processing, 98

cluster analysis, 87

clustered index. *See* index, clustered

COBOL, 190

combined index. *See* index, combined

compound query, 125

contracts, 23, 70, 111

corporate data, 43

corporate document inventory. *See* document inventory

corporate servers, 70

data access, 168

data accessibility, 43

data availability, 167, 179

data footprint, 179

data integrity, 43

data junkyard, 34–36, 37

data model, 110, 149, 166

data warehouse

    architecture of, 42

    benefits of, 43

    defined, 42, 65

    problems with, 44–45, 65

Data Warehouse 2.0

    architecture of, 46–48

    characteristics of, 65

    components of, 49

    defined, 46

    using data warehouse appliance within, 180

data warehouse appliance

    architecture of, 174–76

    benefits of, 177–78

    best practices for implementing, 179–80

    build the unstructured data warehouse using, 180–85

    data distribution across, 176–77

    defined, 173, 186

    history of, 173

    principles of, 173

document inventory, 111–13

documents

    cataloging, 111

    classification of, 113–14

    examples of, 21

    variations of, 114

DW 2.0. *See* Data Warehouse 2.0

email

    characteristics of, 21–22

    ETL example, 91–94

    external criteria of, 147

    retaining original state of, 155

embedded text, 20, 21, 22, 26
ETL. *See* Extract, Transform, and Load
external categories, 69
external categorization, 146–47, 151
external categorization index. *See* index, taxonomy
Extract, Transform, and Load
    defined, 57–59
    email example, 91–94
    engine, 68
    extracting text, 69–77
    loading text, 87–98
    objectives of, 67
    spreadsheet example, 94–98
    structured, 59
    textual, 67, 121–22
    tool, 103, 165
    transforming text, 77–87
    two processes of, 68
font, 81
format. *See* storage format
fractured index. *See* index, fractured
Geo-Spatial Map, 185
granularity, 166
HIPAA, 168, 192
homogeneity, 23–24
homographic index. *See* index, homographic
homographic resolution, 84
hybrid approach, 100–106
index
    alternate spelling, 132
    clustered, 133
    combined, 134
    fractured, 124–26, 135, 140, 159
    homographic, 131–32, 140
    named value, 126–28, 139, 140
    patterned, 130–31, 140

    simple, 123–24, 135, 140, 159
    stemmed word, 132–33, 140
    taxonomy, 128–30, 140
infrastructure, 172
inline additions, 84–85
integration, 59–62, 170, 192
Internet, 70
lack of natural relationships, 32–33, 37
linguistic approach. *See* natural language approach
link
    dynamic, 118
    probabilistic, 116
    static, 119
    strong, 117
    very strong, 118
    weak, 116
medium, 24
metadata, 45, 166, 184, 210
move/remove utility, 87–88
named value index. *See* index, named value
natural language approach, 55
negativity exclusion, 84
NLP. *See* natural language approach
normalization
    challenges applying to unstructured data, 33
    defined, 32
    levels of, 33
OCR. *See* optical character recognition
online application, 40
operational cost, 169
optical character recognition, 70, 102, 170
paper, 36–37, 70
paper tape, 40
patents, 23
pattern recognition, 86

patterned index. *See* index, patterned
Porter algorithm, 69, 81
proximity analysis, 86
punched cards, 40
punctuation, 80
referential integrity, 115
relational structure, 33
Return On Investment, 178
ROI. *See* Return On Investment
Sarbanes Oxley, 33, 57, 85
scalability, 178, 180
SDLC. *See* system development lifecycle
search engine, 27, 70, 81, 173, 207–10, 208, 209
security, 118, 130, 166
Self Organizing Map, 185, 197
semistructured processing. *See* sub doc processing
Service Level Agreement, 167, 179
simple index. *See* index, simple
SLA. *See* Service Level Agreement
SOM. *See* Self Organizing Map
spelling, 31–32
Spider's Web, 41–42, 65
spiral development approach, 100
spreadsheets
    example, 94–98
    limitations of, 22
SQL, 106, 121, 122, 178, 207
stem, 81–82
stemmed words index. *See* index, stemmed word
stemming algorithm, 69, 81
stop word, 78, 79, 88, 91, 103, 124, 135, 158, 185, 196, 208
stop words list, 68
storage format, 24, 33–34, 37
structure, 25–26

structured systems, 49
sub doc pointers, 140
sub doc processing, 135–39
synonym list, 68
synonym replacement, 82
system development lifecycle, 99
taxonomy
    Ablatz, 193
    comparision with data modeling, 149
    complexity of, 171
    defined, 141, 151
    hierarchies within, 147–48
    index, 128–30
    multiple types within, 148
    preferred, 145–46, 151
    preparation of, 102
    recursion within, 148
    relationships across, 143–45
    relationships between, 149
    selecting more than one, 141
    simple, 142–43
taxonomy index. *See* index, taxonomy
text. *See* unstructured data
text characteristics, 23–26
Textual ETL engine. *See* Extract, Transform, and Load, engine
textual integration. *See* integration
thematic approach, 55–56
Tower of Babel, 30–31, 37
transcriptions, 71
transformation, 166
unstructured data
    amount compared to structured data, 153
    analogy to humans, 20
    challenges, 27–37
    characteristics of, 23–26, 26
    defined, 19, 26
    different forms, 20–23, 26

immaturity of handling, 19
querying, 27, 106
variations of, 19
unstructured data warehouse
architecture of, 46
avoiding rework, 157
bridge, 27, 51, 53, 114–16
building small logically
related tables, 161
cake analogy, 64
comparison with traditional
search engine, 56–57
defined, 46, 53, 65
drilling data into sectors,
161–62
factors that shape, 23–26
including embedded text, 22
including spreadsheet, 22
iterative development of, 62,
103, 156–57
justification of, 101

leveraging traditional data
warehouse, 40, 57, 65
methodology, 99–107
mixture of documents, 24
parallelizing the workload,
160
properties of, 54–55
removing extraneous data,
158
screening data, 157–58
selecting the most
appropriate index types,
159–60
use of backward pointers in,
154–56
using data warehouse
appliance to build, 180–85
unstructured system, 50
volume, 24, 27–28, 90–91,
153–54, 165, 170